Richard Brautigan

Twayne's United States Authors Series

Warren French, Editor

Indiana University, Indianapolis

TUSAS 439

83-25290

RICHARD BRAUTIGAN
(1935–   )
Illustration by Alice Notley

Richard Brautigan

By Edward Halsey Foster

Stevens Institute of Technology

Twayne Publishers • Boston

Richard Brautigan

Edward Halsey Foster

Copyright © 1983 by G.K. Hall & Company
All Rights Reserved
Published by Twayne Publishers
A Division of G. K. Hall & Company
70 Lincoln Street
Boston, Massachusetts 02111

Book Production by Marne B. Sultz

Book Design by Barbara Anderson

Printed on permanent/durable acid-free
paper and bound in the United States of
America.

Library of Congress Cataloging in Publication Data

Foster, Edward Halsey.
    Richard Brautigan.

    (Twayne's United States authors series; TUSAS 439)
    Bibliography: p. 134
    Includes index.
    1. Brautigan, Richard—Criticism and
interpretation.
I. Title. II. Series.
PS3503.R2736Z66   1983   813'.54   82-15682
ISBN 0-8057-7378-9

Dedicated,
with apologies,
to those
teachers
who became
my friends

Contents

About the Author

Edward Halsey Foster is an Associate Professor of Humanities and director of the American Studies program at the Stevens Institute of Technology. The recipient of various grants and awards from the National Endowment for the Humanities, Columbia University, and the Fulbright Commission, he has lectured extensively both abroad, under the auspices of the state department, and in this country. He is the author of numerous articles and reviews. *Richard Brautigan* is his sixth book. His seventh will be a critical study of the works of William Saroyan. He is married and the father of two children; he and his family divide their time between New York City and their farm in the Berkshire hills of western Massachusetts.

Preface

Readers too young to remember the literary climate of the late 1960s and early 1970s may be able to read the poetry and fiction of Richard Brautigan with an appreciation and critical objectivity that, for the rest of us, may be difficult or impossible. Of all the major writers who were singled out for attention by the counterculture and who still attract serious attention today—John Barth, Thomas Pynchon, Kurt Vonnegut, Tom Robbins, Ken Kesey, Robert Pirsig, and others—none was more poorly served by readers and critics than Brautigan. Here, it was said, was a writer who, more than any other, had caught the spirit of the age. Like F. Scott Fitzgerald a few generations earlier, he was said to be a man whose work was virtually a history of what it felt like to be alive in America during a period of especially rich cultural intensity and growth.

But Brautigan's best works were in fact never quite what they were alleged to be. Although they certainly do reflect a special time in American history, the time they reflect has little to do with America in the late 1960s and early 1970s. They were, to begin with, written much earlier, although not published until the counterculture had, at least temporarily, become the nation's literary arbiter. At the center of Brautigan's best work is an emotional caution and intellectual reserve, above all a refusal to align with any group or cause, and this is coupled with an absolute individualism, cold and resolute, that could have found no place in the world of communes and easy sentiment that characterized the counterculture, Haight-Ashbury, and "the summer of love." In his lesser works, it is true that Brautigan seemed to respond to his reputation as "an honorary hippie" by writing the sort of whimsical, instantly forgettable fiction and poetry that appealed to many of his readers and critics—but this was long after most of the best fiction, *Trout Fishing in America, In Watermelon Sugar,* and *A Confederate General from Big Sur,* was in print.

The *New York Times Book Review* in December 1980 asked several popular and/or prominent writers what was "happening to fiction," and one of them, John Barth, replied that, unlike the 1960s, there was little interest in truly innovative or experimental writing. That was not altogether a bad thing; as he suggested, much innovative work deserved to be forgotten. But he also noted that the 1960s "was a decade in which so unconventional a novel as Richard Brautigan's 'Trout Fishing in America' could attract a numerous and serious readership."

Barth, of course, is right. The 1960s—and the early 1970s as well—did indeed provide American literature with more of continuing, perhaps permanent, interest than have most periods in American history. It may be that when the final tabulations are made, this decade will find a place beside the 1920s and the 1850s as one of the most accomplished in our literary past.

The problem with the 1960s has nothing to do with the recognition of major writers; it has to do rather with the terms and conditions under which that recognition took place, and it is with this issue that this present study of Brautigan begins. If Brautigan is to be read as anything more than the special enthusiasm of the same group that felt that the Jefferson Airplane and Robert Heinlein represented high-water marks in American culture, the terms in which he has been traditionally read, or misread, must be modified or replaced; otherwise, he can be read only as a survivor of an American cultural phenomenon, the 1960s, that has ceased to have a great influence on the way we live.

The first chapter of the present study, therefore, is concerned with the implications of Brautigan's reception and reputation in the counterculture and then with his earlier—and, in the long run, more beneficial—association with the Beat movement. More important as an influence on his work, however, is Buddhist, particularly Zen, thought, and much of the first chapter is spent suggesting how his acquaintance with Zen may have shaped the special perspective or angle that his narrators adopt toward the rest of the world.

The following four chapters discuss the major fiction—*Trout Fishing in America, In Watermelon Sugar,* and *A Confederate General from Big Sur*—in terms of this perspective and the ways it alters our conventional attitudes toward history and society. In Brautigan's lesser works, as the next two chapters suggest, this perspective is at times compromised in such a way that it seems merely solipsistic or self-indulgent. The last chapter concerns *The Tokyo-Montana Express,* which represents a return to the excellence of the early novels. This most recent of Brautigan's novels shows, more than any other, his special interest in Eastern thought.

Much of the literature valued by the counterculture seems today a dreary wasteland of sentimental and self-indulgent verse, poor science fiction, political rhetoric, and pseudomysticism. But there are major exceptions, works far too imaginative and accomplished to be ignored: the poetry of Ted Berrigan, Ron Padgett, Michael McClure, Gary Snyder, Anne Waldman, and Philip Whalen (to name only a few from this, one of the most astonishingly rich and productive eras in American poetry), Thomas Pynchon's *The Crying of Lot 49,* Tom Robbins's *Another Roadside Attraction,* Robert Pirsig's *Zen and the Art of Motorcycle Maintenance,* and, among many others, Brautigan's three early novels. These works no longer need cult followings to attract either critical or popular attention. It is time to remove the cultural associations that have for so many years influenced the way we have read these books and to see how well, as literature, they stand on their own.

Edward Halsey Foster

Acknowledgments

My first opportunity to deal with Brautigan's work in an extended, critical manner came with an invitation to deliver a series of lectures at various institutions abroad—Hacettepe University, Atatürk University, the University of the Bosphorus, Istanbul University, and the Turkish-American Association in Ankara. This book bears few specific traces of those lectures, but my sense of the objectives and accomplishments of Brautigan's fiction was shaped in the preparation of the lectures and tempered by responses to them. For having made this experience possible, I am deeply grateful to the faculties of the institutions to which I was invited, and I am extremely indebted to Mr. John Challinor, cultural attaché at the American embassy in Ankara, and to Mr. Hüsnü Ersoy, executive secretary of the Commission for Education Exchange between the United States and Turkey. For similar kindnesses, I am indebted to Professors Emil Doğramaci, Sencer Tonguç, Seckin Ergun, and Oya Başak—scholars whose interest in, and knowledge of, American literature is strong and deep.

I am deeply grateful to the board of trustees of the Stevens Institute of Technology, President Kenneth Rogers, Provost Luigi Pollara, and Professor Harold Dorn for having granted the sabbatical during which much of this book was written. Sabbaticals, as every scholar knows, are of first importance in the growth and refinement of good scholarship and its principal reward: excited, informed teaching.

I am grateful also to my students and colleagues in the American Studies program at Stevens who have shared my enthusiasm for American culture of the years from 1955 (Allen Ginsberg's *Howl*) to 1974 (Robert Pirsig's *Zen and the Art of Motorcycle Maintenance*): the new American Renaissance. I am particularly indebted to my colleagues who have shown, both in class and in seemingly endless discussions, that Brautigan is a writer worth our serious, abiding attention: Carol Strickland, Bob Greene, Helen Bauer, John Peacock, Tim Trask, Christopher Zinn, Fred Sugarman, Kay Kier, Jim Cramer, and *above all*, Billy Tracy, who helped more than he may have imagined by politely and delightfully disagreeing with just about everything I said and so forcing me to refine repeatedly just what I felt had to be said about Brautigan. My indebtedness to another good friend, Bill

Goldfarb, now professor of environmental science at Rutgers, is especially great; it was he who first convinced us in the American Studies program to read *Trout Fishing in America* and see it as more than the merely popular novel that it was then widely said to be.

The librarians of Columbia University and Forbes Library in Northampton, Massachusetts—particularly Mrs. Eleanor Shea—were again of immeasurable help in locating every book, article, review, and document, no matter how obscure, that I needed.

I am greatly indebted to Alice Notley, whose portrait of Brautigan was done expressly for this book.

Finally, I would like to thank by name the various teachers to whom this book is collectively dedicated: Nelle Dolan, Horace Thorner, Edward Lawton, Carl Hovde, Fred Dupee, Lewis Leary, Leo Marx, Joseph Ridgely, and Quentin Anderson.

And my apologies, especially to those named above, for the inevitable errors and shortcomings of this book. I hope that there is at least enough good here to convince others that Brautigan is no minor, passing literary fad but rather an authentic and essential American voice from our time.

Chronology

1977   *Dreaming of Babylon.*

1978   *June 30th, June 30th.* Wrote *The Tokyo-Montana Express.*

1979   At meeting of Modern Language Association in San Francisco, appeared on panel discussing importance of Zen Buddhism to American literature.

1980   *The Tokyo-Montana Express.* Began first lecture tour in eight years.

Chapter One

On the Shores of the Pacific

Monterey Pop

In order to understand Richard Brautigan, it is important to remember a few things about the generation or age that made him its literary envoy to the rest of the world. It should be emphasized immediately that Brautigan had less in common with this generation than many— particularly those who did not bother to read his books—once assumed, but it was as a "hippie writer" that he was first read and popularized, and it is here that we should begin.

And if we are to recall that time, we might start with the moment when, according to the media, it all began: the so-called "summer of love." That summer can be dated from the Monterey International Pop Festival, held at the Monterey County Fairgrounds on 16–18 June 1967. Monterey is a short drive south from what was to be the center of the summer of love, the Haight-Ashbury district of San Francisco, and it seemed as if everyone in the "Hashbury" who could pay the admission and hitch a ride made the trip to Monterey that weekend to hear such new San Francisco bands as the Jefferson Airplane and Big Brother and the Holding Company.

But the Hashbury contingent found much more in Monterey than they expected. Monterey Pop was more than a festival of music by San Francisco groups; it was the deciding moment in the creation—with the media as midwife—of the counterculture.[1] A new type of music— the San Francisco sound—was here established as the principal new form of popular music for American youth, and as the music spread from coast to coast, it brought with it the politics, the manner of dress, the customs, and the drugs that separated the hippie culture from the rest of the world. Just as poetry, a decade earlier, had bound the Beat generation together, so music—specifically the San Francisco sound or acid rock, as it was also called—bound a new generation together, gave it a shared interest and identity.

Jimi Hendrix gave his first major American performance at Monterey Pop, and The Who gave one of the best performances that they would ever give. Other performers, all of whom sang and played with intensity and excitement, included the Animals, Otis Redding, Country Joe and the Fish, the Mamas and the Papas, Canned Heat, and Ravi Shankar. The record companies were quick to see that there was a good deal of money to be made here, and any list of popular singers and groups in the following three or four years would contain a large contingent from Monterey Pop. Among those who performed here, Grace Slick, Janis Joplin, and Jimi Hendrix would also have considerable political as well as musical importance, at least within the counterculture.

What surprises us today about the festival—and it is still there to see in D. A. Pennebaker's fine documentary, *Monterey Pop*—is how little of the revolution in customs and dress that began at Monterey was actually *visible* that weekend in the summer of 1967. Viewed today, the audience seems astonishingly neat, well dressed, and conventional. Monterey was no Woodstock, and it certainly was no Altamont. There were no heavy rains, no mud, and apparently no bad drug trips, and yet memories of the festival insist that in many ways it really was revolutionary.

In order to get a sense of the extraordinariness of the festival, we can compare it with a filmed concert held two years earlier, *The T.A.M.I.* [short for *Teenage Music International*] *Show*. The performers at this concert included the Rolling Stones and James Brown, but while Brown gave one of the most powerful performances of his career, the Stones looked very much like prep-school boys on a holiday. And the audience was made up of a generation that could never be confused with the audience at Monterey. If the latter looks neat and well groomed, it also looks relaxed and casual, but the audience at the T.A.M.I. Show belongs to the kingdom of the bouffant hairdo and the party dress. All the girls look like Barbie dolls and all the boys look like her Ken. Mothers may have objected to the type of music performed at the concert, yet there was little cause for concern: the T.A.M.I. Show did not lead to a Woodstock nation—as Monterey did. The mother who had reservations about the Beach Boys, Bobby Rydell, and other popular performers of the early 1960s had real cause for concern only when her son and her daughter started listening to acid rock and then, obedient to the lyrics of Scott McKenzie's popular song "San Francisco," headed west with flowers in their hair. As that mother suspected or knew, her offspring, listening to this new music, flowers in their hair, were also happily ingesting alkaloids. Chemically, as well as musically, they were discovering worlds which she would never know.

With the *T.A.M.I. Show* in mind, Monterey Pop again seems as historically significant as it actually was. The altogether obvious teenage angst and acne of the earlier concert are gone; people really are enjoying themselves now—they are at ease, relaxed. Whether the catalyst was drugs or music or simply the feeling that a new age had really begun, things had changed.

If, however, there was a change, a social revolution of sorts, celebrated at Monterey, it was not permanent, and if it is important to understand Monterey Pop with reference to the T.A.M.I. Show, it is equally important to look ahead a few years to Woodstock and see where the revolution died. Woodstock, despite media insistence that a whole new "nation" had come into being right there on Max Yasgur's farm, gave a benediction to the revolution. In the future, any such "nation" could arise only at the behest of promoters and musicians and their agents. Commercialism had won again; hippies, in their war against capital, had lost. The deaths of Brian Jones in 1969, Joplin and Hendrix in 1970, and Jim Morrison in 1971, together with the violence and murder at Altamont, destroyed forever the naive hopes for universal peace and fellowship that the counterculture had believed would be part of a psychedelic future. By 1969 or, at the latest, 1970, the counterculture as a fact—distinct, that is, from media invention—was dead.

As Hunter Thompson wrote in *Fear and Loathing in Las Vegas* (1971), when Timothy Leary's disciples found that "Peace and Understanding" were not invariably there at

... three bucks a hit ... their loss and failure [were] ours, too. What Leary took down with him was the central illusion of a whole life-style that he helped to create ... a generation of permanent cripples, failed seekers who never understood the essential old-mystic fallacy of the Acid Culture: the desperate assumption that somebody—or at least some *force*—is tending that Light at the end of the tunnel.[2]

As Thompson suggests, there was a clear desire for authority in the counterculture. It was in fact a desire for authority that seems to have reached virtually every corner of their lives—prominently their political assumptions, for as Christopher Lasch has shown, there was little room in their politics for individual initiative.[3] The rebels of an earlier generation, the hipsters and the beats, had cultivated a defensive individuality, but the counterculture cultivated communes. There simply was not enough here to encourage individual convictions outside the community or the general consensus. When the leadership collapsed and things began to sour, the counterculture itself collapsed, and it collapsed fast. Within a year of *Time* magazine's official pronouncement that the Woodstock nation was here to stay, that nation was forever in the past.[4]

But, of course, at Monterey and the Hashbury in 1967, none of this could be predicted. It is possible that one reason for that relaxed, casual feeling at Monterey was that the people there truly believed themselves to be part of a movement or community that was here to stay. The time was summer, the place was California, and the acid was good. Each day brought new arrivals to this new culture. There seemed to be no reason not to expect that things would go on this way forever. The hard and fundamental truth that hipsters and beats had known and around which they had shaped their culture—namely, that there is nothing, in Thompson's words, "tending that Light at the end of the tunnel"—had been forgotten, and someday this would cost the new rebels, the hippie generation, its soul.

But the paradox here is that if this generation had read with care and intelligence the book they claimed was among the very best in American literature—Richard Brautigan's *Trout Fishing in America*—they would, or should, have known that dreams such as theirs never have a chance. In America, as Brautigan knew, the man who does not go along with the dominant culture must, if he wants to survive, stand alone.

Richard Brautigan, Rich and Famous

In 1967, Richard Brautigan was thirty-two, considerably older than most Americans who were making their way to San Francisco and Monterey Pop. He has published a few minor, soon-forgotten volumes of poetry, some copies of which were given away free, and in 1964

Grove Press had published his novel *A Confederate General from Big Sur.*
Some critics liked it, others didn't, and the public was overwhelmingly
indifferent. Generally publicized as a novel of the Beat generation, it
appeared long after the beats had ceased to interest the American
public, and few critics saw any reason to arouse an interest again.

"Poor Beats!" wrote Malcolm Muggeridge in his review of the book
for *Esquire.* "Mr. Brautigan has convinced me that we are better
without them."[5] An anonymous reviewer for *Playboy* decided that the
book was "a surrealist synopsis of everything that was worth missing in
the now-fading beat literary scene," and the distinguished critic Philip
Rahv commented in the *New York Review of Books* that the novel was
"only a series of improvised scenes in the manner of Jack Kerouac. It is
pop-writing of the worst sort. . . ."[6]

And it is here, among forgotten and forgettable beat writers, writing
"in the manner of Jack Kerouac," that Brautigan might have remained
were it not for the publication in 1967 of his *first* novel (first, that is, to
be written, second to be published), *Trout Fishing in America.* The
publisher this time was Don Allen's San Francisco–based Four Seasons
Foundation. A few years earlier, a San Francisco book might have
attracted—like a San Francisco band—very little attention or none at
all. But things were changing. When the Hashbury's new arrivals
sought out books that reflected and confirmed their way of life, they
found *Trout Fishing in America.* In spite of the fact that it was little
advertised, the book sold well, and Allen's company ordered four
printings before turning it over to a mass-paperback producer, Dell
Publishing, who could get it wider distribution. Thousands read the
Four Seasons edition, but hundreds of thousands and then millions read
the aggressively promoted Dell edition. Brautigan's novel was soon as
much a part of the counterculture as the Jefferson Airplane's *Surrealistic
Pillow* and Big Brother and the Holding Company's *Cheap Thrills.*

But there was a paradox here, one which would soon lead those more
interested in literature than in hippies to wonder if this new generation
was really reading the book with real seriousness and attention. Written in 1960–61, its aesthetic design and its politics, insofar as they
belong to any age, belong to the 1950s. It is far more a novel of the Beat
generation than *A Confederate General from Big Sur. Trout Fishing in
America* cultivates in its prose an attitude of emotional and intellectual
detachment that was to be found at the very center of the existential,

alienated culture characteristic of the hipsters and the beats of the 1950s, while *A Confederate General from Big Sur* is *about* people who cultivate this attitude. There is something almost voyeuristic about *A Confederate General from Big Sur*. In that novel, we are asked to watch people in the midst of their detachment from the conventional behavior and rewards (money, fame, social status, and so forth) of civilization, but in *Trout Fishing in America,* we are, in effect, asked to adopt this attitude for ourselves and, for the moment, see the world through its focus. The novel so solidly projects and insists on the ultimate truth and reliability of this attitude that had *Trout Fishing in America* been published at the same time as *A Confederate General from Big Sur,* it might well have been as emphatically dismissed by readers and the critics.

The enormous popularity of *Trout Fishing in America* among American youth may well have had something to do with the fortuitous year of its publication. A few years later, *Time* noted that, at thirty-six, Brautigan had become "an honorary kid,"[7] and with his long blond hair and Hashbury-type clothes, he certainly looked the part. If we look closely at the photographs of Brautigan from that era, however, we do not see a young and, in the jargon of the day, "spaced-out" hippie but rather a clearly middle-aging man behind whose blissful expression seems to lurk an intelligence that is ironic and acute. The pictures do not suggest a literary flower child, but a man of experience, caution, and insight. Jonathan Yardley, writing in the *New Republic* in 1971, suggested, however, that "Not even [Norman] Mailer handles the cult of literary personality more deftly. . . ."[8]

In time, Brautigan came to seem to some people less the literary guru of the hippies than the last hippie in America. His audience grew up, and although many no doubt continued to read his novels, his position at the forefront of writers for the young was soon taken over by such men as Tom Robbins (*Another Roadside Attraction*) and Robert Pirsig (*Zen and the Art of Motorcycle Maintenance*). To new generations, Brautigan's books could seem very dated, old-fashioned—something to be retrieved periodically from the past, like old Jimi Hendrix records or psychedelic posters from the Fillmore West. Brautigan's real value— and it is the contention of this book that he is among the finest writers of our time—*had* to be obscure to later readers who were taught, long before they actually read one of his books, that he was the quintessential

1960s writer. His books could be seen as simply reminders of the way things were and, presumably, would never be again. It was possible to read *Trout Fishing in America* the way that *The Great Gatsby* was often read in the 1950s—less, that is, as literature than as an excuse for nostalgia. It is perhaps the price which, eventually, all books must pay if they are to be interpreted, rightly or not, as essential parts of a particular generation or era. It is the price that John Steinbeck's works paid, and it is the price that Jack Kerouac's are still paying today.

But *Trout Fishing in America,* like Steinbeck's and Kerouac's works, deserves a far better fate and reputation. It is one of the most accomplished, if eccentric, works of the American imagination, and it is time now to extricate it, once and for all, from that age with which it is pervasively associated but to which it never really belonged.

Where He Came From, What He Did

Brautigan was born in Tacoma, Washington, on 30 January 1935. (Considering his reputation as hippie guru, it is appropriate that he was born an Aquarian.) His childhood, to which he refers from time to time in *Trout Fishing in America, Revenge of the Lawn,* and other books, was spent mainly in Tacoma and in Montana. In 1954, he moved to San Francisco, then on the verge of becoming the literary center of the Beat generation. A year later, at a poetry reading there at the Six Gallery, Allen Ginsberg gave the first public reading of *Howl,* and the Beat movement suddenly became a popular phenomenon rather than the private beliefs, pleasure, and literature of a few.

Brautigan had not been drawn to San Francisco by the Beat movement, but he was soon involved with it. He became friendly with Lawrence Ferlinghetti, Michael McClure, and Philip Whalen, a fellow Northwesterner with whom he shared an apartment. He also began to write poetry—as inevitable perhaps for anyone caught up in the Beat generation as learning to play guitar would be for the generation a decade later.

The first of Brautigan's poems to be published, "The Second Kingdom," appeared in the Winter 1956 issue of *Epos*—a Florida quarterly devoted to new poets—and the next year, a selection of his work, together with poems by Martin Hoberman, Carl Larsen, and James M.

Singer, was published in *Four New Poets,* a volume issued by a small San Francisco publisher, the Inferno Press. In 1958, the same outfit separately published his poem *The Return of the Rivers,* and the White Rabbit Press, another small (but rather famous) San Francisco press, issued *The Galilee Hitchhiker.* Similar small volumes followed, but none was issued by major publishers. (Nor, we may suspect, were they intended to make their author rich; in fact, copies of *All Watched Over by Machines of Loving Grace* [1967] were given away free, and the book carries a note to the effect that any poem there can be reprinted as long as the magazine or newspaper or book in which it is reprinted also be given away.)

Although by the mid-1960s Brautigan had a small reputation as a poet, his reputation was as regional as his publishers'. He had considerable competition, too, for it seemed as if *everyone* in the Beat movement was writing poetry. In the ten years following his arrival in San Francisco, he published much, but there seems to be no reason to believe that, had he never published anything more, he would be widely considered a major writer today.

Although Grove Press publicized *A Confederate General from Big Sur* nationally, the book did not, we have seen, create a permanent and substantial reputation for its author. But then came 1967, the summer of love, and the publication of *Trout Fishing in America.* Finally and suddenly, Brautigan was a popular writer. *Life* published a highly complimentary article about him, and other national magazines discussed his books at favorable length. He was asked to read his poetry at Harvard, and his books were reviewed with high critical seriousness (and occasionally high critical sententiousness) in literary journals. At this time, a sure sign that an author had arrived, that he was now "a writer to watch," was having his picture taken by Jill Krementz and published in the Sunday book review section of the *New York Times.* [9] On 14 September 1975, Krementz's photo of Brautigan appeared in the book review. Brautigan had arrived, indisputably arrived.

The Critics Survey the Scene

The problem, of course, was that Brautigan, as we have suggested, had arrived not on his own terms but on the terms of his principal audience, and the disadvantages as well as the advantages of being closely allied to a particular generation would very soon appear. Within a few years of his proclamation as chief literary hippie, Brautigan was widely reviewed and understood as a writer whose primary claim to attention had everything to do with the accidents of time and place. Although some reviewers and critics realized that he owed more to the 1950s than the 1960s—according to one reviewer at the time, "Brautigan [was] a sort of last gasp of the Beat Generation"[10]—others saw his works as literary equivalents of acid rock, love beads, and long hair. The rock critic Robert Christgau, in a generally favorable review, said that Brautigan would "survive as the literary representative of . . . the Hippies," that his "chief competition in the realm of hippie art comes from the Grateful Dead. . . ."[11] The Dead were among the few survivors of the 1960s, and as a rock critic Christgau may have thought it complimentary to compare Brautigan with them, but the comparison was clearly not altogether apt.

From the beginning, many had thought that Brautigan's association with hippie culture was at best a dubious honor. According to a reviewer for *The Times Literary Supplement,* he was "a cult-figure of the American young (by whom, one would have thought, to be praised were no small dispraise) . . . ,"[12] and, in a particularly ungenerous review for the *London Magazine,* Michael Feld concluded that Brautigan's "prose-poetry" was "an eminently greasy brand of psychedelicatessen."[13] A reviewer for the *New Republic* sarcastically announced that Brautigan was "the literary embodiment of Woodstock, his little novels and poems being right in the let's-get-back-to-nature-and-get-it-all-together groove."[14]

Comments like these belong, like the issues of the magazines and newspapers in which they were published, to what now seems a very distant, dated past. Did Brautigan's presumed association with the counterculture, we might ask, really evoke such strong responses? Did critics and reviewers really care? Of course they did, for the literature of the counterculture directly challenged the aesthetic taste of those who had been reared, at least in classrooms, on the New Criticism, T. S. Eliot, Richard Wilbur, and the early Robert Lowell. The reader who had been trained to appreciate verbal elegance and subtlety in works like Eliot's *Four Quartets* and Lowell's *Quaker Graveyard in Nantucket* was not liable to be very happy with those who insisted that rock lyrics were worth serious attention, too.

Two literary cultures have often thrived side by side in America. We should not forget that Thoreau was once dismissed as a misanthrope, and that Whitman was dismissed as obscene, but the opposition of cultural forces in America during the 1960s was especially intense, and Brautigan's books were easy marks for criticism. Going back to that criticism today, we can find much that is certainly valid, much, that is, that can and should be held against his works, but what is more important is the degree to which the less justified aspects of this kind of criticism still shape the way some readers think about Brautigan. If it is necessary as part of our attempt to determine his real literary significance to realize that his association with hippie culture was less than it seemed, it is equally important to exorcise those critical demons that still trail after him and his work: the belief that, all things considered, the best we can say about him is that he is "whimsical," as evanescent and ultimately as forgettable as pleasant moments with good acid or good dope.

There were, of course, distinguished reviewers who insisted that, even as hippie icon, Brautigan might have something worth saying. Anatole Broyard stated in the *New York Times,* for example, that "At his best, [he] is one of those odd-looking guys with long hair and granny glasses who sees, hears, feels and thinks things that makes some of us feel he's found a better answer to being alive here and now than we have."[15] But Robert Adams in a largely generous and warm review for the *New York Review of Books* wrote that "Brautigan has done too much in the genuinely imaginative, powerfully controlled way of vision to be accepted as an artificer of the country cute."[16] Critics could be far more harsh on Brautigan's place among the young. In a lengthy but generally negative assessment for *Modern Occasions,* Cheryl Walker surely spoke for many readers, especially academics, when she insisted that Brautigan was strictly for kids; in "the academy of letters," one read "Beckett, Borges, and Nabokov."[17]

Anyone who in recent years has reconsidered the Brautigan phenomenon of the late 1960s and early 1970s may be more amused than offended by the literary elitism that informed much of the negative criticism that Brautigan's works and reputation inspired. There is an archness and condescension in many of the reviews, both favorable and negative. At times, criticism of his work seems to have more to do with social and political, rather than with strictly literary, considerations. An attack on Brautigan could in effect become an attack on the cultural movement of which he was said to be a chief representative.

But what, after all, could the academy of letters and the more conservative among professional book reviewers say about an author whose poetry appeared with typographical flourishes in *Rolling Stone* (then a much more adventurous and experimental publication than it later became) beside articles on rock, drugs, and social revolution? Clearly this was not the sort of person whose books could be comfortably slipped into the American literary tradition. There was in the first place a question as to just how long there would be a counterculture to admire and read them. The critic, himself in search of an audience, might soon find that he was praising books that, suddenly, no one else wanted to read. "Every day," the owner of a bookstore told the critic Jonathan Yardley, "I expect to come in from lunch and find that the Brautigan cult has vanished in my absence."[18] Whether one were an established critic or doctoral student, it seemed the wise choice to concentrate on a writer such as Beckett (whose work is in some ways similar to Brautigan's) and let Brautigan vanish into that unknown corner of civilization where discarded fads and fashions go. Not every critic felt this way, of course, perhaps not even most, and some of the negative criticisms that Brautigan received were seriously grounded in aesthetic reservations about the books, yet other critical reviews remain to remind us that, for some, the opportunity to review a Brautigan book meant open season on the hippies.

Dissension in the Ranks

Within the counterculture itself, there were occasional grumblings about Brautigan, but here, too, the grumblings could have at least as much to do with politics as with literature. Perhaps the most widely read objection from the counterculture was John Clayton's "Richard Brautigan: The Politics of Woodstock," published in the *New American Review*. What made Clayton's criticisms so effective and widely discussed was that his respect and enthusiasm for the books *as books* was unquestionable. He had, in literary terms, no ax to grind. It was their potential political influence that bothered him. Clayton admitted that he found attractive the imaginative space carved out by *Trout Fishing in America,* but to live there, he knew, would be to desert the barricades in the social revolution in which he and a great many other young Americans firmly believed. "I wonder," Clayton wrote, "is it possible to have both Brautigan's revolution and Che's?"[19] Of course, it was not; one either retreated into the imaginative space of *Trout Fishing in America* or one manned the barricades. No armed revolutions are fought or could be fought in Brautigan's book, at least no revolutions in which the narrator takes part; he is simply too passive—not because he agrees with the world as he finds it, but because he does not seem to feel that there are social revolutions worth fighting. From his perspective, all social purpose is ultimately of dubious value. In the New Left, the political wing of the counterculture, there was good reason to view Brautigan's books with suspicion.

Despite the political objections to Brautigan's works, however, many sympathetic critics immediately ignored or went beyond such matters and insisted on examining the books simply and solely as literature. Tony Tanner wrote enthusiastically in *The Times* that Brautigan was "refreshingly new, unhysterical, unegotistical, often magical" and that *Trout Fishing in America* was "a minor classic."[20] Tanner was especially interested in Brautigan's facility with language, to which John Ciardi, likewise, drew attention; "Brautigan," said Ciardi, "manages effects the English novel has never produced before."[21] The novelist Thomas McGuane wrote that Brautigan's books were "essentially works of language,"[22] and Robert Adams commented that the books were so unlike anything that had ever been written that one could not "call them novels or even fictions—they may well go down in literary history as Brautigans."[23] Another reviewer concluded that Brautigan was "carving out a new syntax, his own geography of the imagination."[24]

On the whole, despite unwarranted and essentially nonliterary criticsm, the verdict on Brautigan's work, especially *Trout Fishing in America,* was favorable, often extremely so. Although his association with the counterculture undoubtedly made his books seem to some people less than admirable, and although within the counterculture itself there were objections to what he wrote, the fact remains that *Trout Fishing in America* and Brautigan's other novels could not be easily dismissed. Whether evaluated in a political context or evaluated strictly as literature, these novels were clearly going to be around for a long time. As one critic in *TriQuarterly* put it, *Trout Fishing in America* might well turn out to be "the *Great Gatsby* of our time."[25]

A New Literature

And yet, despite a critical consensus in Brautigan's favor, major critical issues remained. Although, for example, there could be little doubt that Brautigan was an American author worth considerable attention, how could he be understood within the large patterns and traditions of American literature? Using as a guide merely the literary taste of his best-known audience, he could be grouped with Carlos Castaneda, Robert Heinlein, and a miscellany of other writers. But the relationship between Brautigan and the counterculture was problematic in the first place, and even had it not been, little insight into his work would be gained by grouping him with a sociologist whose reputation derived from a book about an Indian shaman or with an accomplished writer of science fiction who had been around, after all, long before there was a counterculture or even a Beat generation. All that such a grouping would indicate would be that Brautigan's audience had far wider and more eclectic interests than some of its critics liked to believe.

But while there was no easy way to categorize him and while his work looks, on the page, unlike anything any conventional American writer ever wrote, *Trout Fishing in America* and other Brautigan novels sound, in places, quite traditional, not unique at all. His books look like something utterly new, although from time to time we sense echoes of much that we have heard many times before.

In order to understand Brautigan's relation to American literature in general, it may help first to see him together with other writers from his part of the country, the Northwest. That region has, of course, never produced a literature to equal the literatures of New England and the South, but over the years since 1945, it has produced several popular and respected novelists and poets, including Tom Robbins, Ken Kesey, Philip Whalen, and Gary Snyder. These writers share a fascination with mystical, rather than objective or analytical, perceptions of experience. Their works are profoundly influenced by non-Western, or rather non-European, theories and attitudes: shamanism, primitivism, and Eastern quietism, especially as manifested in Taoism and Zen Buddhism. Kesey's *One Flew Over the Cuckoo's Nest* is in part about a triumph of primitivism over the elaborations of Western rationality. When, at the end of that novel, the narrator, an American Indian, escapes from the rigidities and authoritarianism of an asylum and heads north to the land of his fathers, he and his sympathetic readers have turned from the systematic and the rational—for life within the asylum is nothing if not systematic and, within its own terms, rational—toward the primitive and mystic sense of life that his people have known for centuries.

Kesey, Snyder, Whalen, Brautigan, and Robbins appear to have little use or respect for traditional Western rationality and have instead turned to Eastern and Amerindian mystical attitudes and theories of experience as foundations on which to build their literary visions. Whether or not it is appropriate to insist strictly on a regional, literary, or intellectual disposition (since their shared point of view is in turn shared by a number of prominent contemporaries such as Robert Bly, W. S. Merwin, and Allen Ginsberg—writers with few or no ties to the Northwest), the similarities between them do seem to be far more than coincidental. Snyder and Whalen were classmates at Reed College in Oregon and are students and followers of Zen thought; Brautigan and Whalen, as we have noted, shared quarters in San Francisco; Robbins's style, particularly his metaphors, appear to owe much to Brautigan, and *Trout Fishing in America* is prominently mentioned in Robbins's first novel, *Another Roadside Attraction*. If we cannot accurately speak of a "school" of northwestern writers, at least we can say that shared interests and attitudes do set their work off from much traditional American literature.

In the larger patterns of American literature, these writers have much less in common with Henry James, Saul Bellow, and John Updike than with Ralph Waldo Emerson, Henry David Thoreau, and Walt Whitman. They seem far closer to William Carlos Williams than to, say, T. S. Eliot. They are not, in short, traditionalists; they do not fit comfortably into any European-American literary tradition. They seem, rather, iconoclasts, spiritual revolutionaries.

We will encounter Emerson, Thoreau, Whitman, and Williams many times in the following pages, but while we will point out similarities between them, on the one hand, and Brautigan and his fellow northwesterners on the other, this is not to insist on a native tradition for Brautigan. He and, for that matter, the other Northwestern writers are, if anything, their own tradition, too unique to ally themselves with any past. They seem to be less influenced by than simply *like* their predecessors. It is as if *Walden* and *Song of Myself* did not so much influence as *confirm* the mystic vision of these five writers, and that, we may suspect, is exactly the way that Thoreau and Whitman, with their emphasis on the primacy of individual vision, would have liked it. Works like *Trout Fishing in America,* Snyder's *Myths and Texts,* and Whalen's Zen poetry set out to make unique statements about experience, not merely provide variations on the past.

And there are considerable differences between these northwesterners and their American predecessors. Thoreau and Whitman are part polemicists, arguing with their age. *Walden* and *Democratic Vistas* assume that many readers will disagree with what is said. While Robbins's and Kesey's works can be quite polemical, there is little sense in them that readers have to be convinced; the polemics are instead a kind of affirmation of what readers presumably already believe. Thoreau and Whitman set out to teach us; Kesey and Robbins set out to affirm what we already believe to be true. Not surprisingly, all of the northwestern writers whom we have been discussing have become subjects of cults.

Of all American regions, few seem as geographically distinct and provincial as the Northwest. The Northwest is about as far from the centers of economic, political, and, for that matter, literary authority as any place in the United States, and, perhaps as a result, it is also a region which traditionally encourages the kind of absolute self-reliance and desire for solitude that is celebrated in much of its literature. (Those who are not acquainted with this region can get a good sense of this solitude, geographical and psychological, in Robbins's *Another Roadside Attraction.*) In the solitude of those endless rains, mountains, and forests, isolation of the self can become as much a psychological as a geographical reality, and the isolation in turn can enforce a determined self-reliance such as characterizes the people in the fiction and poetry of the northwestern writers we have been discussing. This isolation and determined self-reliance are, in any case, central to Brautigan's work, and while they might be understood as another literary representation, much like, say, Samuel Beckett's *Waiting for Godot,* of the individual's essential, if unchosen, place in the modern world, they may also be understood as the natural effect and expression of that region in which Brautigan spent much of his early life.

Isolation and the Void

It is curious that throughout Brautigan's initial critical and popular reception, the imaginative point from which his fiction and poetry proceeds was rarely commented on or even identified. With monotonous predictability, critics repeatedly mentioned (and continue to mention) his assumed liaison with the counterculture but ignored his regional ties (excepting, of course, his ties with the Hashbury) and his clear interest in mysticism. Cheryl Walker, in an unusually savage attack on *Trout Fishing in America,* insisted that Brautigan was playing a sort of shell game in which his "splash and glitter" prevented his readers from realizing that actually he had nothing to show, that under those shells there was nothing at all.[26] Walker was wrong, obviously; Brautigan is no literary con artist or deceiver. In one sense, however, there *is nothing* under Brautigan's literary shells, for he has certainly cultivated a sense of transitoriness and emptiness in his works. He has, in Gary Snyder's lovely phrase, cultivated "flowers for the void."[27]

That "void" does not result from some private imaginative conceit or from some quiet insolence toward his readers. The "void" in Brautigan's work should be understood in terms of Eastern mystical thought. The "void" here refers to that state beyond rational comprehension which a Buddhist—or, specifically, in the case of Brautigan and Snyder, the Zen Buddhist—considers the ultimate source, of all that is experienced. What we find enacted before and through our senses, according to this perspective, is illusion, insubstantial shadow. True or ultimate meaning lies in, indeed *is,* the great void where, as the source of all things, it is also the source of the very illusion by which it is obscured. By its nature—absolute, eternal, immeasurable—that void cannot be approximated or circumscribed in language; it contains or generates language, and language, therefore, cannot contain it: it is beyond or outside description and definition. The things that, on the other hand, can be described or defined are transitory. As beautiful as these things may appear to our senses, they are, like the flowers in Snyder's metaphor, impermanent, located in an eternal continuum of creation and dissolution.[28]

The seemingly insubstantial or ephemeral nature of much of Brautigan's work—the fact, that is, that it seems so casual, as if it were not supposed to have a lasting value—has its origin in an essentially mystical vision of experience according to which all literature, all art, and, for that matter, all things devised by man are, at their best, "flowers for the void." The impression of permanence and substance that art may give is illusory. If some artists, according to this theory, have sought permanence or stasis in art—namely, that while the natural world is perpetually changing, the work of art is static—the fault is theirs; nothing is truly substantial or permanent—all that we perceive through our senses is illusion.

Zen, it should be remembered, had a considerable effect on the Beat generation, particularly through the writings and personal influence of Gary Snyder and Philip Whalen (who has since become a Zen monk) and through Jack Kerouac's novel *The Dharma Bums* (1958). Kerouac learned about Zen from Snyder, who appears in the novel as Japhy Ryder, and, in his personal life, was deeply affected by it. *The Dharma Bums* has long been respected not only as a novel but also as a sort of self-help manual and introduction to Zen meditation and ideas.

Brautigan has said that he came to Buddhism by accident. When he moved to San Francisco, he met, and was deeply influenced by, people who had made a serious study of Zen. He has said that he learned about Buddhism not by studying it objectively or abstractly but by seeing its effect on others. For all that, the influence, as his work indicates, was profound.[29]

An American Language for Zen

Brautigan shares with Snyder, Whalen, and other American writers influenced by Zen an aesthetic concern for the spontaneous and immediate. Such things matter, so to speak, and any attempt to create a sense of permanence only multiplies illusion: the illusions of experience are compounded by the illusion of permanence. There is little in

Brautigan's work that is reflective, analytical, or strictly intellectual. Although what he writes is often startlingly unique, it never seems complex; it is plain, direct. With the simplest verbal gestures, he devises a world that is intensely felt but instantly perishable. This aesthetic realization would presumably be the result of considerable work, the result of careful working and reworking of language, yet the impression that the finished work gives is much the opposite. It does not seem as if it had been difficult to write, but we need only try to construct typical Brautigan sentences to see how difficult it is. Brautigan's language sounds as if it were easily put together; it is not.

Brautigan's method of composition, however, makes his work *sound* as if it were easily written. He says that he is an expert typist and with an electric typewriter can type out as much as a hundred words a minute. Speaking of his writings, he says that he gets "it down as fast as possible."[30] For those who prefer the precision, craftsmanship, and complexities of the poem or sentence endlessly reworked, his writings can seem too easy, too simple. His language seems to have reached the page too soon; it should have benefited (or so the argument goes) from reflection and revision.

Brautigan's method of composition reminded Bruce Cook, historian of the Beat generation, of Kerouac's technique of spontaneous prose,[31] but Kerouac's prose style could hardly be more unlike Brautigan's. Kerouac's style is elaborate, diffuse, almost baroque, while Brautigan's is spare, his statements clipped. His language, like his insights, is immediate and direct, and yet there *is* much in his prose to remind us of Kerouac's. Kerouac said that he wished to record things exactly as they were at the moment that they happened, and to do that is, for anyone drawn to the Buddhist doctrine of impermanence, the best that one can do. Intellectual reflection, when motivated by a desire to identify principles and patterns underlying experience, leads only to a kind of mystification, the creation of a sense of permanence (the repeating principle or pattern) where there is none. (Indeed what we are doing in this paragraph—identifying certain patterns in Brautigan's prose—is exactly the sort of thing to be avoided.) To claim that things are set and permanent, just sitting there, unchanging, while the writer perfects his description, is to misconceive both nature and art. Since everything, except the void itself, is in an unending state of flux, all that the writer can do, working as fast as he can, is pinpoint a moment in that perpetual transition before it passes forever. As an aesthetic program, Kerouac's technique of spontaneous prose seems, therefore, an ideal extension of Brautigan's vision of experience.

In any case, Brautigan's sentences are neither carelessly nor casually written. If he does get "it down as fast as possible," he does so for good reason. Given the assumptions that lie behind the writing, this method would seem the best way to tell the truth.

Finally, we should add that Brautigan claims that he spends considerable time thinking about or dealing with the things he writes about before actually doing the writing.[32] In this, he would not differ from Kerouac's assumptions behind his technique of spontaneous prose; it is the writing itself which must not be marred by undue reflection or artifice. The subject itself may, as was the case so often in Kerouac's work, have a long history in the imagination.

It does not really matter to most readers how Brautigan writes, what his techniques are, but Cook's suggestion of a parallel between Kerouac's technique and Brautigan's is important. In the end, of course, only the finished book matters—not how it came to be what it is—yet, at the least, this parallel helps us to place Brautigan historically, to suggest that, in terms of literary history, it may be as helpful to see him specifically as a writer of the Beat generation, sharing their techniques and literary theories, as it is to see him in relation to the literature of the Northwest, Eastern mysticism, and the nineteenth-century American tradition represented by Emerson, Whitman, and Thoreau. Brautigan, whom some have considered to be quite unlike anyone before or since, seems to be, on closer inspection, very much within specific literary and metaphysical traditions.

Metaphors in Brautigan's World

Brautigan's critical reputation has always depended largely on his first three novels, *A Confederate General from Big Sur*, *Trout Fishing in America*, and *In Watermelon Sugar*. On the other hand, his poetry, some of it written before the novels were published, has received little attention, and of that which it has received, much has been negative.[33] Brautigan is not a great poet, yet his poetry deserves some attention as the training ground on which he learned to build the metaphors and sentences of his major fiction.

Poetry of Brautigan's sort derives from the work of William Carlos Williams. Characteristically disregarding traditional metrical structures and expressing itself in good *spoken* English, this kind of poetry avoids the ambiguities and linguistic complexities that the so-called "university wits," poets like Richard Wilbur, cultivated in the 1940s and 1950s. In place of complexity and ambiguity, Brautigan and poets like him follow Williams in developing a poetic style that is open, direct, unambiguous, and, in most cases, conversational or rhetorical. It is the sort of poetic style that we associate with poets as different in other ways as Allen Ginsberg, Ted Berrigan, Robert Creeley, and Frank O'Hara. It is poetry to be heard, not deciphered. Ideally it can immediately affect the man who hears it rather than send him scurrying off to the library to study it, to unravel slowly its structure and sense. Plainness and immediacy are the desired effects. It is clearly a type of poetry that can fit well with Kerouac's compositional technique (which in fact had much to do with certain developments of the type) and with Brautigan's interest in Zen.[34]

From the beginning, Brautigan's published poetry has been of this sort. However eccentric its subject, it is syntactically and verbally "easy" to understand. There are never the kind of syntactical complexities that we find, for example, in Lowell's early poetry, and the words are always taken from common speech. In *The Galilee Hitch-Hiker* (1958), for example, Brautigan says that the poet Baudelaire, running a hamburger stand, served people flowers instead of the hamburgers they expected,

> . . . and the people
> would say, "What kind
> of a hamburger stand
> is this?"[35]

Poetry like this is undemanding and charming in a wholly ephemeral manner. By some standards, of course, it is not poetry at all but merely prose that has been divided up into lines that do not necessarily even have the distinction of being separate syntactical units. The division of lines does not seem to have any meaningful point or purpose. Indeed, a later work, "A Moth in Tucson, Arizona," was originally printed as a paragraph in *Five Poems* (a broadside issued in 1971) but was rearranged as a stanza of poetry in *Loading Mercury with a Pitchfork* (1976). Nor does it seem to make much difference *how* the words are arranged; the effect is substantially the same whether the words *look* like prose or like poetry.

Basically, Brautigan's poems are carefully constructed sentences. His language, as we have seen, is characteristically spare and direct, and, much of the time, all that the poetic *form* (lines and stanzas) seems to do is draw attention to the language itself. We tend to read or listen with greater attention when the finished work looks like, or is said to be, poetry. In effect, the poetic form in Brautigan's work insists that we listen or read closely, but it does relatively little to modify or manipulate a poem's indigenous sense.

Although poetic form in Brautigan's work is of minor interest, his literary sensibility is decidedly poetic—as much in his fiction as in his poetry—because of the basically metaphoric nature of his expression. His work can be most effective when he approaches his subjects not discursively or narratively but metaphorically. His type of metaphor is his own, allowing a sense or impression of fleetingness or insubstantiality—the opposite, that is, of the impression which metaphors, usually grounded in solid visual and aural imagery, are supposed to give. Traditionally metaphors are used to fix or establish meaning; they are a form of nondiscursive definition. We take from them more-or-less fixed impressions, or definitions, that could not be reached through common literal discourse.

But not in Brautigan. His metaphors seem always to be caught in a perpetual process of simultaneous creation and dissolution of sense,[36] and he thereby approximates his special Buddhistic vision. Bordering on the ineffable, his metaphors seem to dissolve as soon as they are apprehended. Rather than establish meaning, they establish transitoriness as a fundamental component of knowing. Nothing is ever at rest; meaning is seldom permanently fixed.

"1942," originally published in *The Octopus Frontier* (1960), provides an especially fine example of this technique in its third verse. The speaker refers here to his uncle . . .

> twenty-six years old, dead
> and homeward bound
> on a ship from Sitka,
> his coffin travels
> like the fingers
> of Beethoven
> over a glass
> of wine.

The poem obviously does not exist in any commonly recognizable spatial or, despite the poem's title, temporal context. Brautigan splices two sets of images (coffin, fingers) together, gets his metaphor, and immediately deserts it. Without any spatial or temporal parallels between the images and with little resonant or musical language—such assonance and consonance as there are, are negligible—the images that have been fused in the construction of the metaphor separate fast and go their separate ways. Having no roots in our conventional world of shared experience, the metaphor has, in a sense, no place to settle. Only the syntax, apparently, makes the metaphor possible. Whatever similarity Brautigan may have hoped to suggest through the metaphor exists far outside our usual range of sensual and intellectual apprehension. The metaphor and the similarity it documents flower for a moment and, finding no correlation in our everyday world, vanish—"a flower for the void."

Brautigan's metaphors may remind us of the bizarre associations common in surrealism, but the surrealist metaphor achieves its effect first and foremost through apparent incongruity, and it is the incongruity that stays with us. But while there is a certain incongruity or illogicality in Brautigan's metaphors, it is not this which strikes us first. Brautigan's metaphors do work; in their way, they do make a kind of sense, but the sense lies in the region of mood, not in visual or other sensual similarities. And like the moods, the metaphors are evanescent; they can dissolve and disappear rapidly.

But this is in no way to belittle Brautigan's achievement. For a brief moment, he has evoked a poetic sense where none existed, and it is a sense that, true to Zen vision, is only transitory, momentarily viable and meaningful. On the other hand, when these metaphors are massed together—as they are in *Trout Fishing in America*—they have a collective force that is both metaphysical and aesthetic. The individual metaphors are individually no more resonant and lasting in the large work than in the short poems, but the vision that informs them remains; that, at least, will not go away. The metaphors, ephemeral in themselves, have their particular and lasting value as keys to the vision that made them possible. Repeatedly shown to us, the vision stays—as it might not after the short poem—while the metaphor, which, after all, is only a kind of carrier, is forgotten.

Perhaps it is because Zen vision is so unusual in our world, so unlike what most American literature offers, that many critics, searching for a word to express their own reactions to Brautigan's language, have called his work "magical." And it *is* magical, for against all logical odds, it gives the lie to that rational order which most of us consider inevitable and integral to experience and nature. Our shared mode of rational comprehension is profoundly questioned.

It is essential to realize that Brautigan's vision is not simply a matter of language, that his metaphors are not merely whimsical exercises with words. Brautigan has often been praised for his facility with language,[37] but what is most important about that language—its supreme achievement—is its ability to point the way through a territory that does not allow the sort of description and definition that usually characterizes literature.

If a Brautigan poem finally works, it does so because it evokes a vision, a way of seeing. Here is a good example, "The Nature Poem," originally published in *The Octopus Frontier* (1960). Juxtaposing, as usual, unexpected (and bizarre) images, Brautigan begins by comparing the moon with Hamlet, at night, riding a motorcycle:

> He is wearing
> a black leather
> jacket and
> boots.

I have
nowhere
to go.
I will ride
all night.

Like so many other Brautigan poems, this may at first seem only another surrealistic exercise, but it is much more than that. The motorcycle, like the man—always changing, always in motion— embodies the Zen vision of a world in perpetual transition, but it is transition full of violence. Hurtling through the night on his motorcycle and dressed in motorcycle boots and leather jacket, the motorcyclist is in this image of violence paradoxically at rest with the world. There is no tension between the rider and what he is doing. Robert Pirsig in *Zen and the Art of Motorcycle Maintenance* (1974) similarly used the motorcycle and its rider to suggest the lack of tension, the easy fit, between two objects in motion—and to the same purpose: Pirsig and Brautigan both suggest that the motorcyclist, always in motion but without destination, intuitively expresses in his being what the disciple of Zen knows—that the world is continually changing and that the change is without logical purpose.

Using Brautigan's language, we can say that those who, like the motorcyclist, accept or intuitively express the Zen principle of eternal change will know that he has "nowhere to go." Since the world is shadow, illusion, it must also be without final meaning or destination. In "The Nature Poem," the Zen perspective is realized in a metaphor that, like the motorcyclist, will vanish eventually, leaving behind only the perspective that made it (and his act) possible in the first place.

Where Do We Go from Here?

Poetry provided essential training for Brautigan's later work. In particular, it taught him how to construct the kind of sentences he wanted, and when he felt he had accomplished this, he turned to fiction and wrote the major works on which his reputation rests.

But he continued to receive little encouragement, at least financial encouragement, from critics and readers. Between 1965 and 1968, his writings earned him less than $7,000. In 1966, he was appointed poet-in-residence at the California Institute of Technology, but, unlike many other contemporary poets, his reputation and income would have little to do with academia.

As we have seen, his support came the following summer. Flower children would do much to make him famous, a media star with his photograph in *Time* and *Life*, but for the present, Brautigan—as a disciple of Zen culture with a wholly unique sense of language and experience—would be largely misunderstood.

Surely few people that summer could have foreseen how inappropriate Brautigan's association with the counterculture could be. And even fewer could have guessed how ephemeral and transitory the counterculture's influence, especially in literature, would prove. The message of the festival at Monterey was simply that the future looked good, and that message was so fervently preached and believed that even proverbial skeptics found themselves converted and, for the moment, running with the pack.

Chapter Two
Intimations of Apocalypse
A Novel of New Manners

Trout Fishing in America was written before *A Confederate General from Big Sur,* but the latter was published first, and a reader coming to terms with Brautigan's work would be wise to start here. It is a more conventional novel, easier to read and easier to understand. Stylistically less eccentric, it can also serve as a gloss to ideas and attitudes that *Trout Fishing in America* deals with in somewhat greater detail and depth. *A Confederate General from Big Sur* is related to *Trout Fishing in America* in a way reminiscent of the relationship of Hawthorne's sketch "The Customs House" to *The Scarlet Letter.* Although the narrative and factual content of the first has little to do with the second (and in fact was written afterwards), thematically "The Customs House" is closely linked to the novel and was originally published as an introduction to it. An understanding of Hawthorne's thematic objectives in the sketch contributes much to an understanding of the novel. If we can understand the thematic intentions of *A Confederate General from Big Sur,* we are on the way to interpreting his similar, but far more complexly stated, intentions in *Trout Fishing in America.*

In one sense, *A Confederate General from Big Sur* is simply a novel of manners. The principal details of character and plot resemble very much the sort of things we would expect to find in novels by Louis Auchincloss and James Gould Cozzens. The book's narrator, Jesse, is a theological student, and he tells us a series of related episodes involving his life in San Francisco and at the home of his friend, a general named Lee Mellon, at Big Sur. Other characters include Johnston Wade, a wealthy businessman from San Jose, and Mellon's girl friends Susan and Elaine, daughters of eminently respectable families. Susan's father is a businessman in San Francisco; Elaine's is a lawyer.

But if Jesse, Lee, Johnston, Susan, and Elaine sound at first conventional, they are conventional people in unconventional times. In another time or place, they might have become quite ordinary and respectable middle- or upper-middle-class people. But today they are distinctly out of place. Their values and lives, however conventional they seem at a distance (Lee embodies the spirit of pioneering self-reliance, while Jesse views experience in distinctly moral ways) seem peculiar in the context of America today. Even the flower children who made the novel so prominent and popular must have found Jesse and Lee a little bizarre.

Lee Mellon is a general, but he is a general only on his own authority. He did not graduate from West Point or any other military school, and he has no commission. He is, furthermore, a general for the Confederacy—a hundred years too late. Lost causes are his specialty.

Mellon's friends are no less extraordinary. Susan has two objectives in life—babies and movies. When not giving birth, she likes to spend her time at the movies. Elaine is interested in little except sex and dope, and Johnston Wade, the suffering victim of a bitchy wife and neurotic children, has become a certified psychotic. Another of Mellon's friends, Elizabeth—temperamentally the most normal of the group—is a truly gentle woman who lives much of her life either contemplating spiritual matters or raising her four children, but she also spends part of each year in Los Angeles as a highly paid, highly skilled prostitute.

Jesse, to no one's surprise, is at times disconcerted or astonished by Lee Mellon and his friends, but even in the midst of this unexpected assortment of individuals he can seem rather bizarre himself. He is, as we said, a theological student, but only in the sense that Lee Mellon is a general. Jesse's current interest is the punctuation—periods, commas, semicolons—in the book of Ecclesiastes.

Jesse, Lee, and the others are pariahs, outcasts—not by choice but inevitably by reason of their failure or refusal to behave in some acceptable or expected fashion. If Johnston Wade were willing to be only what his wife and children want—a source for money and nothing more, certainly not a man with ideas and values of his own—he could survive in a conventional way. It is the desire to be someone different or perhaps something *more* than society permits that has made them outcasts. Their only prominent shared characteristic is their inability or unwillingness to conform. Given what they are, they are, in this world, troublesome or simply unnecessary.

These people are not outside society because they want to be; they are unintentional rebels with nothing to defend but their integrity, their sense of themselves. They are not misanthropes by choice, and if there were a church for Jesse, a way for Lee, and a devoted family for Johnston Wade, they might seem utterly ordinary. But there is absolutely no chance that this will happen, and so they must spend their lives in a kind of psychic struggle for survival. Elizabeth travels to Los Angeles, earns enough to support herself and her children, and returns to Big Sur, free again. She and the others gain a small measure of dignity and considerable integrity in their insistence that they be, insofar as possible, only what they think they should be.

Mellon's War

The novel evolves as a series of interrelated episodes rather than as a single narrative. The first section of the book involves episodes in Lee Mellon's life in San Francisco and Oakland, and the second section involves episodes during Jesse's visit to Lee's home at Big Sur. The book is narrated by Jesse, but what he provides is only a series of loosely related anecdotes and observations. The novel's subject, as the title indicates, is Lee Mellon, and little is mentioned unless it tells us, if only by contrast and implication, something about him. The other people are essentially variations on the character—the rebel by default—of which Lee Mellon is the type.

Mellon says that his grandfather was a Confederate general at the Battle of the Wilderness, that crucial battle during which Grant, despite catastrophic losses, decided to press southward. In time, this decision brought the Confederacy to its knees. The Battle of the Wilderness was the turning point of the war; the luck of the South had run out. In Lee Mellon's personal version of the battle, however, it was a fine time to be a Confederate general, especially for his grandfather. Tradition, Mellon says, has much to say about his grandfather's heroics, including one episode in which, with a single blow from his sword, he decapitated a Northern soldier.

There is, however, no official record of a Confederate general named Mellon in this battle—or, for that matter, anywhere in the war. Jesse suggests, with nothing but family tradition to back him up, that Grandfather Mellon was actually a private and that the Northern soldier had lost his head before the grandfather saw him. Grandfather Mellon was barefoot and, in his sole encounter with the soldier, stole his boots. According to Jesse's account, Lee Mellon's grandfather was a coward who was deserting his comrades and the South at the time he discovered the dead soldier and got his new boots.

Lee Mellon and Jesse decide to find out the truth. They get from the library a copy of Ezra J. Warner's *Generals in Grey* (an actual book, a scholarly treatise published by a southern academic press), but it tells nothing of a man named Mellon serving the Confederacy. Lee is certain that the book is wrong, and he asks his friend to promise that he will believe that Confederate General Mellon is no myth. And Jesse promises. After all, there really *is* a Confederate general named Mellon—not the grandfather, of course, but Lee Mellon himself. The fact that he was born somewhat late to fight in the war is beside the point; he is a Confederate general to the core, marching about San Francisco in his uniform. He is, Jesse says, "a Confederate General in ruins" (18).[1]

But if there really is a "Confederate General from Big Sur," the Southern cause has already been fought and lost, and so Lee Mellon is a loser even before his first military campaign. But that, of course, is no reason not to *try*; he "lay[s] siege to Oakland" with "a daring calvary attack on the Pacific Gas and Electric Company" (49)—which is to say that he illegally taps the gas lines for his own use. He gives up the siege, however, and retreats to Big Sur when he is unable to pawn a stolen electric iron. (Thievery, not bravery, is the most obvious characteristic that Lee Mellon and his grandfather share.) But at his country home—an architecturally unstable, unintentionally surrealistic nightmare, put together from odds and ends with no blueprints—he finds a new enemy, one far easier to attack and conquer: frogs. He emerges from the battle a victor, having vanquished his enemy with a troop of mercenary alligators.

If Mellon's campaigns will not find their way into many accounts except Jesse's, it is also clear that if there were a real war to fight, Mellon might very well emerge an effective leader. Certainly he would prove a vicious one, for while he can be, within his limited means, a good and generous man, he can also be inhumanly cruel. Any man foolish enough to make Lee Mellon an enemy would find an opponent as vicious as the mythical grandfather who decapitated the Northern soldier with a single blow. For example, when Mellon is propositioned by a homosexual, he does not just walk away; he bashes the man on the head with a rock, steals his watch and money, and goes off with the keys to the man's car. When Mellon discovers two teenagers trying to steal gasoline from his truck, he threatens to shoot them. The gun, as it happens, is empty, but none except Mellon knows this, and his victims are driven hysterical by his all too credible threats.

At another time, Mellon, whose attitude toward woman—fuck 'em and shuck 'em—is in perfect keeping with his character, deserts his girl friend in return for a twenty-dollar bribe. When she returns, pregnant with his child, he will have nothing to do with her and pretends not to know her when they encounter each other on the street.

And there is much more that is equally unpleasant or reprehensible. He repeatedly treats people in vicious and inhuman ways. Without compassion for anyone, he might well be an effective, certainly a ruthless, leader on the battlefield.

In the end, it is his pointlessly cruel attitude toward Johnston Wade that destroys his friendship with Jesse. Wade is a psychotic, the victim, as we have seen, of a thoroughly unpleasant, truly contemptible family. They have no use for him; they care only for his money. Wade is, at the least, a pathetic man, a man to be pitied, but Mellon treats him no better than his family did. At one point, Mellon chains him to a log so that he will not get into trouble. "It was just horrible," Jesse says (142).

Wade is too confused to understand just how cruelly he is being treated; it seems to him as if he received far worse treatment from his wife and children, but while their cruelty lay primarily in ignoring him (except when they wanted the bills paid), Lee Mellon has set out actively to hurt or humiliate the man. In a bleakly comic episode, Wade says that the log to which he is chained is a fine companion in his sleeping bag: it reminds him of his wife. When Jesse speaks to Mellon about the way Wade is treated, Mellon says simply and casually that there is nothing to worry about, and at that moment, Jesse becomes fully aware of his friend's capacity for cruelty and feels, he says, "a sudden wave of vacancy" come over him (148–149).

Mellon comes by his cruelty naturally and, in a way, honorably, for he is, Jesse claims, "The end product of American spirit, pride and the old know-how" (93). Mellon is as sure of himself and as self-willed as Americans are proverbially said to be, and in addition, there is something of the western outlaw or desperado in his makeup. There is also something of the "robber baron"—every inch a gentleman among friends, every inch a ruthless oppressor among enemies. Mellon's home may be an architectural nightmare, but when there, he can as much play the role of gracious host as could the wealthy owner of a Newport estate. He may treat Wade with unconscionable cruelty, but he also makes a point of calling him "sport," which recalls the generous, but emotionally empty, hospitality of the title figure in F. Scott Fitzgerald's *The Great Gatsby.* For Jay Gatsby, "sport" was a handy word with which to address guests, especially when he could not remember their names. Like Gatsby, too, Mellon is interested first in pursuing his goals, whatever the human cost. Anyone who gets in the way gets hurt.

Mellon also enjoys pretending to be an intellectual. (To continue the parallel with Gatsby, we might remember that Fitzgerald's character has a well-stocked library, but it is all for show; Gatsby does not actually read. He, like Mellon, is far more interested in appearances.) Mellon reads such Russian authors as Turgenev, Tolstoy, and Dostoyevsky, although writers of such intense moral purpose are strange choices for one with such a limited sense of moral imperatives and compassion. He also reads Kant, Schopenhauer, and—at last an appropriate choice—Nietzsche. Perhaps we are supposed to assume that he understands little that he reads or at least is little affected by it. The important thing is to impress others—and perhaps himself.

Rebel Without a Cause

Mellon is no intellectual, but his life seems to be a strange series of echoes from American literature and myth, particularly the literature and myth of rebellion. His illegal tapping of the gas lines in Oakland, for example, parallels an episode in Ralph Ellison's *Invisible Man* where the setting is New York and the victim is the electric company. In both cases, men get exactly what they want and need despite the rules, regulations, and bills of American business. (The parallel, as Terence Malley points out in his book on Brautigan, is not exact, however, for Ellison's hero succeeds in his enterprise, while Lee Mellon cannot quite control the gas and winds up with a flame six feet high.[2])

In his limited moral sense, Mellon is the negative of Thoreau, but in self-willed poverty at Big Sur, Mellon does remind us of Thoreau's experiment at Walden. At his cabin, Mellon has little that he does not need. He has taken Thoreau's dictum—to simplify his life—as seriously as Thoreau himself did. There is nothing extraneous at Big Sur.

There are echoes of *Moby-Dick* as well, for Mellon has, like Ishmael, willfully ostracized himself from the world. At Big Sur, he likes to spend time watching whales swimming out in the ocean. (Jesse adds that he would not be surprised to see them decorated with Confederate flags in their spouts.) The sentence with which the final chapter begins—"The Pacific Ocean rolled to its inevitable course . . ." (105)—may echo Ishmael's statement near the end of *Moby-Dick*: ". . . the great shroud of the sea rolled on as it rolled five thousand years ago."

Whatever Mellon's faults, and they are many, he is also an adventurer, a pioneer of his own dreams. He is, in Jesse's words, "a kind of weird Balboa" (105), a conquistador in search of a life that, paradoxically, only he can define or create. He is another in a long tradition of such American heroes as Natty Bumppo, Ishmael, Huck Finn, Jay Gatsby, Tom Joad, and Sal Paradise—men who cannot accept the world as it is and so transform it, or at least what they know of it, into what they envision and need.

Although seldom really likable, Mellon is very much a comic figure. (We suspect, for example, that even if he did not choose to live like Thoreau, he would *have* to live that way; he is too inept to succeed at much besides poverty.) Even as a comic figure, he belongs in a class with such characters as Huck Finn. Fundamentally, such people, aside from their vision and dreams, are ordinary people; it is the strength of those visions and dreams, which for Mellon involve martial glory, that distinguishes them. In this fashion, Brautigan's novel suggests, an American raises himself out of the commonplace.

The self-willed American rebel and visionary to whom Mellon has the closest links is the one popularized by movies in the 1950s: the rebel without a cause, the innocent victim who retains fully his sense of the way the world should be. Mellon is, of course, literally a rebel without a cause, for it is Brautigan's joke that Mellon is a Southern rebel long after the cause has been lost and forgotten, but he is also in his lethargic way—for surely few American rebels have had as little energy as he—the kind of rebel portrayed by James Dean, Marlon Brando, and others in films of the 1950s. These rebels were in conflict with the shallow standards, self-righteousness, and hypocrisy of their communities. They were not rebels by choice; they had no revolutionary ideas or programs to follow. Their rebellion was only a way of keeping themselves and their sense or vision of the way things should be uncorrupted by their communities—communities which in turn considered this nonconformity as sign or proof of criminal intention. But these rebels did not consciously intend at first to hurt or even to change their communities. They simply withdrew from them, and the anxieties and anger which were in part both the cause and the result of this act found their outlet in violence or the threat of violence, of which the motorcycle commonly became both the symbol and the type. In *The Wild One*, for example, the motorcycle gang, always restless, always on the move, does not intend any violence; they want only to be left alone. But they are *perceived* as being violent and iconoclastic, and the community puts them into situations where, unless they act contrary to their natures, they must be violent; they must either take revenge or compromise themselves.

Mellon is frequently on the verge of explosive violence. He always has the potential for unrelenting cruelty but he never seeks out violence; his victims, like Johnston Wade, force themselves on him—never the other way around. Like Brando in *The Wild One* and James Dean in *Rebel Without a Cause*, he would prefer solitude to compromise; he would rather live alone than compromise himself. When the outside world invades his privacy—as it does when the homosexual tries to proposition him and when two teenagers try to siphon off his gas—he attacks with incredible violence. Left to himself, this characteristically American rebel—a man with no ideology, no politics, no real worldly ambition—survives well enough; it is the world which transforms him into the truly disagreeable, unpleasant man that he seems to be throughout most of the book. Mellon, like the Old South, is always and only on the defensive.

Henry Miller and Thomas Wolfe are among famous American rebels mentioned in the book. Mellon grew up in Asheville, North Carolina, which was both Wolfe's home and the setting for much of his fiction. Henry Miller makes a personal appearance, sitting in his car waiting for the mail to be delivered to his home at Big Sur. But these rebels from the 1930s are Mellon's predecessors, not his contemporaries, and their rebellion would have been too programmatic, too intentional for Mellon. Wolfe and Miller were perhaps rebels as much by design as by temperament. Theirs also seems to have been a literary kind of rebellion, for whatever they experienced soon became grist for fiction. That certainly was not true of the rebels played by Dean and Brando, and it is not true of Mellon.

Mellon, in other words, is a particular kind of rebel from a particular age. He is a natural or existential rebel; his rebellion is an end in itself and is its own justification. He may live near Henry Miller and have been born in Thomas Wolfe's town, but Brautigan, by including these facts, merely points out differences between the rebels of two different times and circumstances.

The rebel without a cause is always a loser; there is no way that he can topple the community values that try to mold and oppress him. Numbers are never on his side. But Lee Mellon is the extreme—the loser's loser, who has made of his condition an art. He is too lazy to be efficient or to try anything that would make him a productive and agreeable member of the world around him. Like a would-be Johnny (the character Brando plays in *The Wild One*), he has a motorcycle, but it is strewn about in dozens of pieces, waiting to be put back together. But it is extremely unlikely that it will ever be reassembled; that would require too much work. Mellon is without the ambition or skill to be anything except his inefficient self; he could not be violent toward anyone who had not provoked him—he simply does not have what it takes. And yet while others are continually compromising themselves by accepting majority values, he does succeed admirably at being himself. It is a comic success, of course, but it is still a success; he does not change the world, but the world does not change him. Mellon does not criticize the world for not providing him with what he wants (a Civil War, of course); he simply deserts the everyday world and sets up his own reality: a war with the noisy frogs at Big Sur. Much as we may dislike him, we must admire him at least for this: he survives.

Mellon's Wonderland

Lee Mellon's vision of the way things should be permits just about anything that he wants, and as long as his friends and visitors are with him, they, too, have the ability to transform experience into whatever they desire. He is the grand doyen of a magic empire in which the rules of "the real world" are of marginal or no importance.

Of course, it helps to be drunk or high on dope. The day in San Francisco that Jesse meets Mellon for the first time, they buy some whiskey, find an alleyway, and get drunk together, and from that time forward drink as much as their limited means allow. Mellon, in spite of his poverty, is well supplied with marijuana, and at the end of the book, he, Jesse, and their girl friends are soaring high, "poleaxed by dope" (154).

Even when they have no liquor or dope, Mellon and his friends are able to construct private wonderlands out of a vast variety of suggestions from movies, comic books, and other kinds of popular culture. When, for example, Johnston Wade arrives at Mellon's house, his host and Jesse decide that he looks like Roy Earle, the man played by Humphrey Bogart in *High Sierra,* and it is as Roy Earle that Wade is known throughout the rest of the book.

Jesse tells us that he likes to take in three movies at a time at a cheap theater, and it is as a movie that, in several respects, he sees his own life and the lives of those around him. He narrates the book in a series of brief, intensely visual episodes. There is little analysis in his account; like a film, it is continuous motion, a montage of actions. Movies influence the substance, as well as the form, of his narrative; among other things, Jesse dreams about Alfred Hitchcock (an appropriate figure when your companion is Lee Mellon), acts as if he were in a western, and remembers Mellon in the aftermath of a drunken bout as if reviewing a scene from a movie (146, 76, 90).

Like the movies, the world that Mellon creates and shares with his friends is magic. Anything can happen here, even a replay of the Civil War, and so it should be no surprise to the reader that the white rabbit from *Alice in Wonderland* makes an unscheduled and otherwise inexplicable appearance (68, 108). He simply hops by, Jesse tells us, and disappears—no explanation and no further connection to the story.

Mellon's wonderland makes the bizarre seem normal. In another time or place, Elizabeth might seem exotic, but here there is no discrepancy or disparity between her surroundings and the way she chooses to lead her life. It is not at all out of keeping with Mellon's wonderland that she can work part of the year as a prostitute and yet be a spiritual, intelligent, gentle woman, so gentle indeed that she is a vegetarian because she will not be the one responsible, however indirectly, for killing animals.

Lee Mellon's wonderland is suffused with his potential for violence, but, paradoxically, private gentle lives are possible here that are not possible in the far more violent world outside. And that may be why people are attracted to him. The boundaries and possibilities of his life and the lives of his friends stretch and expand in his kingdom in ways that simply would not be possible, would not be permitted, elsewhere. The apparent opposition of values in Elizabeth's life might have to be resolved in "the real world," where consistency is valued. In Mellon's world, however, she can be exactly what she says she is, and as long as she does not interfere with the private visions and sensibilities of others, as long, that is, as she respects others as much as they respect her, she will be among friends. No one there, at least, would want it otherwise.

What the World Does to Us

The people whom Mellon admits to his wonderland are often reminded of what life on the outside is like, but they are too far removed from it, both geographically and imaginatively, to be altered in any serious fashion by it. In fact, it is the outside world that is likely to change when it comes into contact with Mellon's world. The change may result simply from his predictably violent reaction to the intrusion—but not always. Among those who accidentally stumble into this wonderland, for example, is an elderly grandmother in her chauffered Rolls-Royce who wants to see the Big Sur country but who is afraid that, if she does, she will not arrive at her grandchildren's at the time they expect her; but then, having crossed the boundaries into Mellon's world, where what matters has little to do with the expectations of others, she decides that being late might be a good thing: her grandchildren have been taking her for granted long enough. She will take her time.

Another visitor from the conventional world for whom this wonderland means freedom is Johnston Wade, successful businessman (the Johnston Wade Insurance Company) and formerly devoted husband and father. He has done all that he can for his family, but their only reaction has been to expect more. They are astonished and offended when, at the age of fifty-three, their breadwinner buys a sportscar; he must, they think, be mad—which, thanks to their ingratitude and demands, is exactly what he is. But like the elderly grandmother, he does not have to account for his actions, or at least the actions for which he is sanely responsible, in Mellon's wonderland. (When he goes off the deep end, of course, Mellon treats him as any other obnoxious visitor would be treated and ties him to the log.) In Mellon's world, Wade does not have to apologize for what he is.

The real world is always right there—right next to Mellon's domain—and it is always intruding itself, only to be transformed either by his violence or his visions. As cruel as Lee Mellon can be, he has the imaginative power to make life far more bearable than the real world can. As Wade knows all too well, Mellon's war games are less vicious and inhuman than the social games and expectations back home in San Jose.

Jesse's Version

Mellon and his friends at Big Sur are, Jesse tells us, economically just hanging on. They have little food and little money to buy more. Perched on the shores of the Pacific, they are, figuratively and literally, on the far edge of America. In some respects, they seem to be nothing so much as protohippies—hippies, at least, before the word was invented. It would obviously be wrong, however, to conclude that in showing us Mellon's wonderland, Brautigan was only doing advance publicity for hippie communes.

For much of the counterculture, rebellion was defined in terms of style, particularly in matters of behavior and dress. Moral behavior could also be seen as style, always relative to the specific time, place, and circumstance. There was not even a fully articulated, generally accepted, and viable political position; had there been, the counterculture might have been around much longer than it was.[3] The counterculture, after all, was in large measure a reaction to the dark side of American life—poverty, racism, and, above all, the war in Vietnam—but Mellon and his friends do not merely react to that dark side; indeed, Mellon's pleasure in violence connects him directly to that dark side; he would love a war.

Mellon and his friends are not adopting a style; they are simply and persistently themselves. Nothing can make them compromise with their time and place; nothing can make them behave the way they are supposed to behave. But they are not really reacting *against* the world around them; nothing in that world has very much, either good or bad, for them. They are neither arguing nor agreeing with that world; they are simply being whatever it is that they are, and as a political program (unintentionally political, of course), nothing an individual could do would be more powerful, more damaging than this. It is civil disobedience carried to its logical, furthest extreme, but Mellon, who theorizes about nothing at all, probably would not understand that. He did not learn about civil disobedience by reading Gandhi or Thoreau; he learned about it simply by insisting on being himself.

Mellon seems to be the ultimate expression of self-reliant, individualistic America, but is Mellon—the man who transcends the accident of his place in time, the man who is absolutely the man he wants to be, not what the world insists he should be—supposed to be an actual man or is he rather Jesse's imaginative fiction? There is finally no way to answer the question satisfactorily; our only evidence is the evidence that Jesse gives us—we know only what he chooses to tell. *A*

Confederate General from Big Sur is finally his book, his vision of history and the way it is, or could be, transcended. Lee Mellon is only the example.

Jesse tells Elaine that he is a minister, but although in a sense he is joking—since he has no congregation (except his readers) and there is no indication that he has formally studied theology or been ordained—in another sense he is not. He is as much a minister as Lee Mellon is a general. If "Lee" is a good name for a Southern general, "Jesse" is certainly appropriate for a minister; the historical Jesse was the father of David, Israel's great king, and traditionally is believed to have been the first in the family from which St. Joseph was descended. Although Jesse has no church, he is, in a special way, a man of God and may understand more of the spiritual life than many of his ordained brethren.

When Jesse reads the Bible, he reads Ecclesiastes. He tells us that he used to read Ecclesiastes several times a night, then once a night, and then a few verses a night. Finally, as we noted earlier, he decided to concentrate entirely on the punctuation—which is a decision far more logical and sane than it may appear at first glance. Ecclesiastes, aside from references to the will of God, is unable to give us any purpose or explanation for life, and in a world without ultimate meaning, counting punctuation marks can be as appropriate as anything else—more appropriate than most things, perhaps. It is an absurd act for an absurd world.

As anyone closely familiar with Ecclesiastes must realize, it also provides a sort of cosmological explanation and justification for Jesse and Lee Mellon's plight as men outside their time. According to Ecclesiastes, ". . . the race is not to the swift, nor the battle to the strong, neither yet bread to the wise, nor yet riches to men of understanding, not yet favors to men of skill, but . . . chance happeneth to them all."[4]

This passage should have been inscribed over the entrance to Mellon's home at Big Sur, for he and his friends have been denied the very rewards that should have been theirs, at least to their way of thinking. Certainly Mellon himself would have been an effective, which is to say cruel and determined, officer if history had permitted. And if the battle should have been his, riches should have been Jesse's, for he *is* a man of understanding, a man who knows why things are the way they are. But his reward is not riches but rather the understanding itself— understanding the world well enough to know that, first of all, since "chance happeneth to them all," those who are deserving will not necessarily get their rewards.

Jesse also knows that there is value and meaning beyond the injustices of day-to-day life. If there is no rational, ordered system of justice, there is an order that transcends human control or manipulation; as stated in Ecclesiastes 1:9, "The thing that has been, it is that which shall be; and that which is done is that which shall be done. . . ." It is a vision of endless repetition and a refutation of the alleged influence of temporality, progress, and change. In essence, Ecclesiastes asserts that, although giving an appearance of change, things really do not change, in any final or ultimate way, at all. The universe, correctly understood, is endless motion, endless repetition.

Jesse and Lee Mellon are extremes—the man of peace and the man of war—and what Jesse emphasizes, primarily through metaphors, is that whatever they are doing has been done before. These extremes are endlessly repeated. Brautigan's characteristic literary device is used here to cross through time and geography to suggest similarities or parallels between one era or incident and another. At first, these metaphors may seem merely whimsical or humorously ironic, but once Jesse's fundamental assumption—that despite change, nothing really changes—is understood, their real purpose is clear. When Jesse says that Lee Mellon lays siege to Oakland, retreats to Big Sur, and captures Wade, his prisoner of war, he is not being merely ironic (although, of course, he is being that, too). His frequent references to the Civil War and to war stories—chapter titles include, for example, "In the Midst of Life" and "A Farewell to Frogs"—have their humorous and ironic purpose, but they also serve larger ends. In his own (small) way, Mellon is as much a tactician as a real general, as resourceful and, on the whole, as successful. He does, after all, succeed in whatever he undertakes. If what he undertakes is of little consequence (except to himself), the fault must be attributed to history, to the conventions and expectations of the way we live now—certainly *not* to any lack of ambition.

In the prologue, Jesse quotes from *Generals in Grey* to show that Civil War generals came from just about every possible occupational background (doctor, minister, Indian agent, civil engineer—you name it), and they could expect just about any fate (assassination, suicide, death from natural causes, death on the battlefield). Among Confederate generals, there were few common denominators except for the fact that they happened to be in the right place at the right time. Lee Mellon does not meet that condition, but the obvious point is that neither would any of these generals if they were around today and, like Mellon, favored the Confederacy's cause.

Again, the obvious conclusion is that any type of individual might be found in any place at any time. It is the time and the place that are seldom right for the individual—not the other way around. The insistence that people can be, and that Jesse and his friend are, inappropriate to their historical situation is a fundamental assumption on which the novel is built. "Our names were made for us in another century" (78), Mellon says to Jesse, and he perhaps could have gone on to say that their characters and values were, too.

The feeling that an individual should not be understood primarily as a function of time and place, as a psychological compromise between public and private needs, but rather as a self potentially and ideally independent of history underlies Brautigan's best work. The detached, ironic intelligence that results from a refusal to accommodate one's self to one's historical situation, and a refusal to accept on faith the opinions of the majority, is the point where the political and social satire of *Trout Fishing in America* begins and also provides the principal subject of, as well as the narrative point of view for, *In Watermelon Sugar*.

Although Jesse says that he is a minister, he never says that he is a Christian, and his point of view is in fact distinctly not Christian. Having chosen Ecclesiastes as his text, he has decided to focus on one of the most eccentric, least representative books in the Bible. With that particular book's vision of ceaseless repetition—for reasons inscrutable to all but God—it will not fit the Christian insistence on linear time—the movement, that is, through history from man's fall to his eventual damnation or salvation. Ecclesiastes insists that, in the end, God shall judge, yet it also insists that, in our world, there is no justice, no inevitable cosmic principle, except life itself, on which to rely.

The student of Zen, rather than the student of Christianity, should see much of interest in this inability to find justice as a coherent and ultimate principle in the universe. This conclusion goes far to justify that nonjudgmental, dispassionate awareness which is cultivated by the Zen disciple—and which is also fundamental to that view of experience that we find throughout Brautigan's work. Jesse, it is true, does judge others, but he does so dispassionately, as if aware that there can be no finality in anything. He is still in a position to hedge his bets. He is certainly not a Zen mystic, but in his detachment from things and his inability to view the universe progressing in a coherently logical, linear, and just fashion, he approaches that sublime awareness that the Zen mystic knows.

Solutions

And so what can a person do; how can he organize his life; how can he find purpose or meaning or at least motivation for it? What he primarily finds in Ecclesiastes, after all, are explanations, not solutions.

If there is a solution, it may lie, at least for men like Jesse, in the imaginative creation of wonderlands like Lee Mellon's—wonderlands well fortified, if necessary, by alcohol and marijuana. Drunk or high, Mellon and his friends—although faced with the fact that as far as the rest of the world is concerned, they are without much value—never have reason to despair.

Given a choice, Jesse and Mellon might well prefer dope or alcohol to sex—particularly sex that brought with it any further commitment. At one point, since Mellon is too drunk to sleep with his girl friend Elaine, Jesse does; he will keep her happy—that is all that matters. At another time, when Elaine tells Jesse that she wants to make love, he agrees to it, but without any personal interest. Once again, he will keep her happy.

In the book's final scene, Jesse can find neither the interest nor the energy for sex. Elaine says that he has been smoking too much dope, but it is just as likely that, in view of his previous indifference to her, one more time with her would be one time too many. Men like Jesse may be more interested in their private visions than in any close personal relationship. They are far beyond a lasting desire for friendship, so they stand alone, justified by their private selves and their private ambitions.

All that they ask for is a wonderland like Lee Mellon's, or, barring that (and by the end of the book. Mellon's wonderland, because of his repeated cruelties, has collapsed into a nightmare), all that they ask for is solitude.

Autonomy

There is no real community at Mellon's place—only a collection of miscellaneous individuals with little in common except the fact that they have even less in common with the rest of the world. There is, heaven knows, no consciously articulated political purpose at work here, no enforced sense of a collective enterprise. Politics—despite the fact that, as we have seen, Mellon's wonderland, by ignoring the rest of the world, takes in effect a political stance toward it—have not so much been transcended as ignored. With such a strange group of individuals, any communal effort would be expected to fail. If the guests at Big Sur do more or less what their host wants—when he has the energy to want anything—it is only and simply because the property is his—which is about as primitive, and as conventional, a reason for authority as one could find. But sooner or later, people like Mellon's guests will, given their extraordinary independence, object to any authority, and that, of course, is exactly what happens when Jesse objects to Mellon's cruel treatment of Johnston Wade. Finally, a community is, for men like Jesse, not a permanent possibility, but even without a community, he, Mellon, and friends will probably survive. Their senses of themselves and their imaginative resources are too great to be violated or destroyed by the world around them.

A Confederate General from Big Sur is concerned with a kind of rebellion that goes much deeper than political theory, much deeper than any collective or communal purpose. This rebellion involves a transcendent awareness in which politics have no part. Mellon's role as a general and Jesse's as a minister would ordinarily entail social obligations; in fact, it is social obligation which largely defines what the general and the minister have to do. But Jesse and his friend are as free of human expectations as they are free of history. In addition to solitude, they require autonomy, the freeing of their individual selves from all but self-imposed restraints. The cost is high, for there is no feeling that this autonomy is necessarily a good thing, personally or socially. Neither Jesse nor Mellon is especially happy in his respective freedom, and, as Jesse knows, the freedom that his friend's autonomy provides *can be* not at all welcome. It might be appropriate to subject Mellon to a good deal of social restraint; what the world surely does not need is another general, with or without a war. In a world of transcendent independence, there is a man of war like Lee Mellon for every man of peace.

Jesse, who has willed himself free of the restrictions of politics, time, and place, would undoubtedly agree with Emerson that "Nothing is at last sacred but the integrity of [one's] own mind,"[5] but he would not share Emerson's optimism, his belief that integrity of this sort will inevitably put one on the road to sublime moral enlightenment. He knows that giving the highest value to this sort of integrity can imply the survival of all the violence and cruelty that history and politics, at their best, have tried to overcome. Jesse's position here is close to the profound ironic pessimism of Hindu thought in its insistence that, by transcending history, one does not transcend evil any more than one transcends good. In Christian theology, it can be argued that God, for reasons beyond man's understanding, allows evil to exist and thereby justifies it—it is all we know and all we need to know. But if this is so, it may also be assumed that evil, with God's grace, can be transcended; that, after all, is the message of Christian salvation. For Emerson, trained originally as a minster, this assumption could be, and apparently was, transferred to his private and otherwise non-Christian religious speculations, and the assumption has been passed down to American religious systems, such as Christian Science, that have been influenced by transcendental thought. But Jesse insists on standing outside that tradition. However much an Emersonian he seems in his commitment to freedom, solitude, and autonomy, he is finally closer in his thinking to the Orient than to anything that could have reached him by way of Concord, Massachusetts.

In transcending history, Jesse knows, *a man does not transcend moral dichotomies*; indeed, that transcendent act only sharpens them, as the dichotomy between Jesse and his friend is sharpened in the course of the book. With the complications and ambiguities of history gone, the dichotomy stands in primitive clarity.

Similarly, the differences between one's self and the world are not resolved, although they may be obscured, by Jesse's kind of transcendent vision. His solitude is not temporary or conditional. It is absolute; there is no turning back, and sooner or later, his refusal to deal with the world on its own terms will get him into trouble—if nothing else, then mundanely and forcefully in the form of the IRS.

There is no better evidence of the social conflicts that Jesse's vision invites than his relationship with women. In one sense, it may seem that Jesse and many other Brautigan narrators and heroes are as much misogynists as Lee Mellon is. But to believe this would be to miss the point. There is no misogyny here; women are not being treated as inferior—in this world, beyond a certain point, they simply are not needed. If the highest achievement is to be alone, to protect one's integrity, then it follows that no one, certainly not a girl friend, is absolutely necessary or necessarily desirable. No other judgment is intended, but that, of course, is probably not the way it will be perceived by others. And so Jesse and his friend choose women like Elaine for their companions, women, that is, who are thoroughly unpossessive. If Mellon is available, that is good, but if he is not, Jesse will do just as well.

In America, Alone

A Confederate General from Big Sur, says Jesse, has 186,000 endings a second—in other words, the speed of light. In Einstein's equation, $E = mc^2$, the speed of light is assumed to be the only constant in the universe, and everything else is relative to it. The novel is also about constant, invariable factors: namely, the infinitely replicable, but substantively unchanging, factors that make people what they are. There are seemingly unlimited possibilities or endings for any given moment; anything (or any one of 186,000 things) could end Jesse's book, yet whatever does happen has happened before. The possibilities of experience, it may be, are the constants, like light, to which the individual is relative.

Jesse gives us five of the possible 186,000 endings, and all five suggest similar ideas. In the first of these endings, he tells us that what he and his friends are doing is exactly what they are destined to do, that it is inevitable; in the second, he emphasizes that whatever happens now has happened before, a fact specifically noted by comparing the present moment with old photographs; and, in another ending, Johnston Wade, throwing hundreds of dollars into the Pacific, says that money has finally done nothing for him but bring him to this moment. In these various endings, in other words, there is a repeated insistence on fate and inevitability and on the fact that whatever happens has happened before. The novel ends with resignation, an acceptance of experience and its underlying laws without any desire or wish or hope to change what is; while Jesse may transcend history, he does not change it or condemn it. It is, coming from a deeply religious man like Jesse, a specifically mystical acceptance, one which, as we will find, is characteristic of all Brautigan's major fiction.

A *Confederate General from Big Sur* is Jesse's essay in what true, determined freedom entails, and this, of course, has been a persistent concern of major American literature. *The Adventures of Huckleberry Finn, Moby-Dick,* and *Walden* immediately come to mind as books which share Brautigan's concern. That the book owes more to Eastern thought than to traditional American definitions of freedom is beside the point: they all begin at the same place. It is really America and American freedom with which Jesse, if for no other reason than the accidents of time and geography, must concern himself, however indirectly. But ultimately, Jesse knows, freedom is no national possession; true freedom, imaginative freedom, is available anywhere.

Having said that, it is still no coincidence that Jesse's ultimate awareness and resignation take place on the farthest reach, geographically and intellectually, of contemporary America. What Jesse has reached may also be the farthest outpost of the American imagination. Similar settings serve similar functions in many American works— Nathanael West's *The Day of the Locust* is a good example—and, given Brautigan's essentially metaphoric and symbolic imagination—it is likely that he intends us to interpret it in this manner.

America has crossed through time and space to the Pacific, and, having reached the geographic limit, what has been gained, at least metaphysically, except a new version of what has happened countless times before? Do we now know only what the author of Ecclesiastes knew and what Jesse knows: that "the thing that hath been, it is that which shall be . . . and there is no new thing under the sun" (1:9). There is in *A Confederate General from Big Sur* an unsentimental, stoic vision of America as historically less but metaphysically more than we expected—a vision in which there is no historical *progress* but in which all possibilities can be realized. America may encompass all possibilities, but it cannot add to those possibilities anything essential that did not already exist. What America does, in other words, is confirm what we already knew; its final value is not creative but, in the best sense, monumental.

Good Manners

This chapter began by suggesting that *A Confederate General from Big Sur* in broad outline resembles a conventional novel of manners but that the resemblance is only superficial. Manners, after all, are historically relative, and perhaps the best thing to do with them is what Jesse and Lee Mellon and friends do: ignore them.

In keeping with our diminished present—a present in which the individual is increasingly hedged in by social conventions and expectations—we err in judging individuals *solely* in terms of their historical function, which is to say their accomplishments and their manners.

Jesse, as we have said, compares Mellon with Balboa, but while both found the Pacific, one was looking for riches and fame and the other was content if he could find enough cigarette butts to make a new cigarette. Jesse's comparison seems only momentarily silly or ludicrous or even whimsical. The fact that history has provided Lee Mellon with such impoverished opportunities tells us everything about history and nothing about him. And that, in effect, is what Jesse discovers when he sees how vicious his friend can be; a determined individual like Lee Mellon is free of history, and the error lies in judging him according to the changing possibilities and customs, the manners (in a broad sense) of a specific era.

The ending of *A Confederate General from Big Sur* is reminiscent of Samuel Beckett's *Waiting for Godot*. In Beckett's play, two men as historically ineffectual as Jesse and Lee Mellon are waiting for someone named Godot who will bring with him an answer or solution to their human dilemma—that is, their inability to give meaning to their lives—but we are certain (or as certain as we are of anything in that uncertain play) that Godot will never arrive. Brautigan's novel similarly ends with Jesse's hard-won knowledge that there is nothing to wait for, no ultimate explanation. Whatever is, is here already, and it was here from the very beginning. To know that, we have only to extricate ourselves from the present, to invite solitude and autonomy—at least in our imaginations.

Chapter Three
Politics in North Beach

Chaos for Sale

As we know, the generation that made *Trout Fishing in America* a best-seller packed concert halls, stadiums, and the great outdoors to hear the Grateful Dead, Jefferson Airplane, and Big Brother and the Holding Company. What the Grateful Dead and others were to music, *Trout Fishing in America* was, it seemed, to literature—a nice thing to have along when high on dope. If the book seemed disorganized, if it did not make much sense, that was all right—it really was; you could open to any page and find something funny, and that was the thing that mattered. This generation, which high-school teachers had taught to analyze, if not enjoy, *A Tale of Two Cities, Julius Caesar,* and other chestnuts, found suddenly a literary work that, without readily discernible plot, characters, or theme (nothing to analyze!), was fun to read. If it were like anything, it was that literary find of an earlier rebellious generation, William S. Burroughs's *Naked Lunch,* the chapters of which, rumor had it, had been shuffled in no particular order and published just like that. Like *Naked Lunch,* Brautigan's novel, funny as it was, looked utterly chaotic—a great virtue for a generation which authoritatively condemned authority, reason, and order as enemies of all that was good.

In fact, despite its reputation, *Trout Fishing in America* is very reasonable, ordered, and authoritative. Far from being the whimsically chaotic book that, with good dope, it seemed to be, it is extremely *artful,* and nothing about it is more artful than its apparent pose and celebration of artlessness. In its language and arrangement of chapters, it may initially seem a grand gesture of literary anarchy, a return to the intentional disjunctions and innocuous chaos of Dadaism: all the rules of good literature appear to have been thrown to the wind—as indeed in a way they have been—but as a closer look suggests, *Trout Fishing in*

America, unlike Dadaist works, has been built according to rules no less restrictive than those which they replace.

It is the essence of Brautigan's style to appear observant but uninvolved, casual, and—in the jargon of California and the late 1960s—laid back, but the choice, especially the economy of choice, and the arrangement of words and chapters is exacting, precise. He gives us a wide range of verbal devices—metaphors, aphorisms, slang expressions, and so forth—in order to evoke an America of which we were always aware but which we had never known quite so well.

Brautigan's prose *documents* America. It is a personal testimony, a record of what is, and behind it can be found the authority of Walt Whitman's well-known assertion, ". . . I have no mockings or arguments, I witness and wait."[1] In Brautigan's prose, American things are seen as they are—they are witnessed, documented—and Brautigan, without judging them (except insofar as selectively pointing at them is itself a kind of judgment), lets them judge themselves. Nothing is made to seem more or less than it is; nothing is heightened or exaggerated merely for comic or dramatic effect; nothing is seen with anything but the cool, neutral eye.

The ability to see things as they are, not judging them by making them appear better or worse than they are, may in part tell us why, in the late 1960s, pervaded as that period was by a well-founded distrust in authority, those who read the book closely enjoyed it as much as those who did not; for there was no sense of *instruction* here, no sense that the book, however satiric and political it seemed, was supposed to *teach.* The satire in the book derived from America's own internal contradictions rather than its inability to measure up to the standards of someone's ideological presumptions. Satire here was not a literary convention; it was a fact of American life. Because the book did not insist that its readers share with it a political framework, it could be a source of delight for anyone who, regardless of his politics, viewed the goings-on in Washington and southeast Asia with increasing despair. The reader brought politics to the book, not the other way around.

The disengaged, thoroughly nonpolitical narrative voice in *Trout Fishing in America* is effectively the voice that Jesse develops at the end of *A Confederate General from Big Sur*—that is, the nonjudging, emotionally unattached voice that implies an awareness of the fact that the truly transcendental self indiscriminately accepts evil as well as good, Lee Mellon's martial cruelty as well as biblical revelation. Jesse does not try to change Lee Mellon or, for that matter, try to change anything; that would be beside the point. From Jesse's panoramic, transcendental perspective, decisive change is impossible, for the evil inevitably returns. From his perspective, Jesse strictly records—in this case, 186,000 endings a second—and recording is, likewise, what the narrator of *Trout Fishing in America* does. These narrators, or at least their narratives, are like cameras that trigger themselves, setting down, in documentary fashion, what is and leaving moral interpretations to the rest of us, the readers. Among American writers, the obvious parallel is, again, with Whitman: "Evil propels me and reform of evil propels me, I stand indifferent."[2]

Similarly, for Jesse and the narrator of *Trout Fishing in America,* evil is accepted, if not condoned, as being as much an inevitable expectation of experience as good. There is no judging "person" here—the narrator of *Trout Fishing in America* has no name and no real character; he does things, but without projecting a "personality." We are, in short, not listening to an individual's opinion; the authorial voice is beyond that and speaks from such a totally abstract position that evil can, like good, seem simply real, its own justification.

Clearly this authorial voice, utterly dispassionate and objective, is a fiction, for a close study of the book suggests that there is actually a good deal of personal, authorial involvement and judgment going on. Although the authorial voice would have us believe that it is doing no more than passing on to us exactly what was witnessed, in fact through metaphors, juxtaposition of materials, and so forth, it is clearly constructing a very personal image of America. On the other hand, if we do not at least recognize the central assumption of the novel—that America is judging itself, not being judged by the narrator—we will miss the reason the book seems so authoritative, conclusive.

The narrator of *Trout Fishing in America* gives us no more reason to trust him than does the omniscient narrator of, say, a Dickens novel. We simply must believe in him, for without that belief his observations will merely seem idiosyncratic, something whimsical but not necessarily reliable or true. And if we believe that, the book may seem only an amusement or distraction. But in the case of *Trout Fishing in America* it is particularly important to accept the narrator as a reliable authority. In a Dickens novel, the narrator's credentials are accepted on the basis that there is no one but he who can tell us what we are told; *Trout Fishing in America*, on the other hand, suggests that it tells us only what we would find for ourselves if we could dismiss our prejudices and preconceptions and look a little closer.

Brautigan's narrator should not be understood as a person with conventional strengths and limits or even as an omniscient authorial voice in the traditional sense. He is much more than either—or at least that is what he is supposed to be. Because of our very lack of personal involvement, except the most tangential,[3] with the narrator, because, it seems to us, he has nothing to lose and nothing to gain by portraying America one way and not another, we trust him implicitly.

But should we? However abstract, disinterested, and detached the narrator seems, the narrative itself is shaped with precision. There is nothing accidental or inevitable about the narrative; there is obviously a controlling intelligence behind the material and even behind the authorial voice. The fiction of a narrator who has nothing to lose and nothing to gain can blind us from seeing how artfully he—or his creator—has arranged what he has to say. To understand *Trout Fishing in America* critically, we must understand first its shaped aesthetic and political vision and then understand the function of the narrator in making that vision seem not a version of the truth but rather the truth itself.

Trout Fishing in America and its narrator do not really document America. What they document is a highly selective vision of America, and therein lies, as we will find, a unique appropriation of Zen theory that Brautigan's Buddhist readers may be disturbed by but that, on the other hand, gives the book, as literature, increased fascination.

"Insist on Yourself; Never Imitate"

No word, not even "magical," has been used more often than "whimsical" to describe Brautigan's fiction, but "whimsical," like "magical," is not a critical term that says or helps much—nor is it, despite its ubiquitous appearance in favorable reviews of Brautigan's fiction, a wholly complimentary term. It limits the work in unfavorable ways, removing the work from the realm of "serious" literature. Emerson in "Self-Reliance," it is true, said he would carve "whim" on the lintels of his door-post, but in his own life and in his writings surely few men could have been less whimsical than he. Whimsical things are generally without much purpose or great value; they are oddities, curios—pleasant enough in their own way, but generally without ongoing interest or wide application. They may divert us, but they do not sustain interest very long. If the word is understood in a limited way as meaning "pleasantly unconventional," it is an acceptable way to describe Brautigan's work—but it is not useful in any important or revealing way.

In any case, *Trout Fishing in America* is a very closely, although unconventionally, organized book. At first it does seem (although never unpleasantly) chaotic, disorganized, random, fanciful—even whimsical. It is like the rides at an amusement park, full of pleasant, unanticipated surprises but, also like those rides, perfectly, mechanically ordered. Like them, it is a work of considerable engineering and structural finesse, but unlike them, its end is not merely to divert, not to be classified with the things we might do, so to speak, on a whim.

Trout Fishing in America is supposed to be a novel—at least that is what the title page says—but it certainly does not look like a novel, and the very attribution can become ammunition for critics who would, while liking and praising the book, dismiss it as "whimsical," as less than serious, or, at best, relegate it to that literary Sargasso Sea occupied by Laurence Sterne's *Tristram Shandy* and other books that do not fit conventional assumptions about what a novel should be. For anyone interested in literary traditions, that classification is good enough reason to dismiss a book, as F. R. Leavis dismissed *Wuthering Heights,* as a "kind of sport."[4]

And certainly a reader or critic should be forgiven for failing to discover an adequate way to classify this seemingly miscellaneous collection of essays, sketches, observations, and anecdotes. Many of the "chapters" appear to have little to do with anything else in the book except that they deal, like the rest, with one or more varieties of what is called "trout fishing in America" or, occasionally, "Trout Fishing in America." But is trout fishing in America a thing or a label or a person or a disguise? We never really know, for at one point or another, it could be any or all of them. It appears as a political slogan, a hotel, and a man. A ballet and a cookbook are created for him (or her or it). The narrator learns about trout fishing in America from his stepfather, later meets Trout Fishing in America, talks with him, and shows us his letters. He even gives us a report of Trout Fishing in America's autopsy which suggests that in some vague, indeterminate way Trout Fishing in America is like Lord Byron.

We are also told about a wino named Trout Fishing in America Shorty who rides around San Francisco in a wheelchair. The narrator would like to pack him up and ship him to Nelson Algren in Chicago, but Trout Fishing in America Shorty becomes a movie star instead. There are many varieties of trout fishing in America, but since they are introduced in such an apparently casual, pointless, artless fashion, they can seem to have very little, if anything, to do with each other—or, for that matter, with anything outside the book at all.

And what could be more whimsical than that?

Perhaps here we have the basis for an explanation for the book's phenomenal popularity. *Trout Fishing in America* seems to belong by itself; it seems to have nothing, at least nothing practical, to do with anything *but* itself; and within itself, all is delightful disorganization. It provides a fine escape from a world where everything is altogether too ordered. The book must then exist for fun and diversion no more serious than a Ferris wheel or the dodge-'em cars.

Outlines and Maps

Trout Fishing in America has forty-seven sections or "chapters" (chapters only by virtue of the fact that they are distinct thematic units, not because any fundamental narrative division is indicated).[5] Seven of these chapters—numbers 1, 10, 21, 28, 33, 37, and 40—deal with the North Beach section of San Francisco, that part of the city where the Beat generation and its activities were most in evidence, and six chapters—2, 3, 5, 18, 26, and 35—deal with the narrator's childhood. Finally, eighteen chapters are about the narrator's fishing trips: 4 ("Red Lip"), 7, 8, 11, 15, 16, 17, 20, 23, 25, 27, 29, 31, 34, 36, 38, 39, and 42 ("Footnote Chapter to 'Red Lip' "). Since the book is not plotted in any traditional way, any of these three divisions can be removed from the rest of the book and discussed independently. The chapters dealing with the fishing trips are narratively consecutive, but this is only obliquely apparent, since Brautigan, as we will see, emphasizes a series of related metaphors rather than narrative continuity. Few of the chapters in the other divisions narratively follow from each other; they are linked through metaphor and theme.

Chapter 43 ("The Cleveland Wrecking Yard"), a vision of America as a vast business and junkyard, is the book's true conclusion, the remaining four chapters forming a sort of coda and benediction to everything that has preceded them. The chapters which do not fall into these divisions—North Beach, childhood, fishing trips, conclusion, and coda—are miscellaneous essays and anecdotes which elaborate in rather unexpected ways ideas in neighboring chapters. These miscellaneous essays and anecdotes include "The Autopsy of Trout Fishing in America," "Another Way of Making Walnut Catsup," and so forth.

When chapters are not consecutively arranged according to narrative requirements, they are arranged according to subject with chapters that contrast with, or complement, those which precede and follow them. This arrangement of chapters is often ingenious, and one of the more mechanical pleasures which the book provides is unraveling the reasons for the arrangement or order of chapters. For example, chapters 17, 18, and 19, although at first glance quite dissimilar and unrelated, deal in some fashion or other with political terrorism of especially gentle varieties. In the first of these chapters, there is a shepherd who looks like a "friendly" Hitler (34),[6] and his sheep keep getting in the narrator's way. It is easy to deal with that sort of terrorism; eventually the sheep will go away, and eventually they do. (At the chapter's end, the narrator receives a message simply stating, "Stalingrad." Like the Nazis in Russia, the sheep are in retreat [36].)

The next chapter deals with an incident in which the narrator and his friends were involved in the sixth grade. They chalked the words "Trout fishing in America" on the backs of first graders—a nicely innocuous form of terrorism but terrorism nonetheless—but the principal of the school interfered, the words were removed, "and a kind of autumn fell over the first grade" (46). In the last of the three chapters, Trout Fishing in America (a man this time) reports that FBI agents have been scouring a trout stream in search of a certain fisherman—although why they are doing this (and failing) remains as much a mystery as why the sheep keep getting in the narrator's way or why he wrote "Trout Fishing in America" on the backs of first graders.

The three chapters are from three of the different divisions mentioned above—respectively, fishing trips, childhood, miscellaneous incidents and essays—but they work together to form an unexpectedly amusing impression of a world in which everyone is involved in an elaborate, but not necessarily malevolent, game of terrorism or authority—an impression that is reinforced in various other chapters throughout the book. We repeatedly encounter victims and victimizers, and the victims, we should not be too surprised to learn, are often trout. We may be reminded here of Lee Mellon's battle with the frogs at Big Sur and Jesse's realization that people like Mellon, whose battles are generally trivial and amusing (although somewhat less so when his victims are people), lack only the opportunity to be much more and much worse. One of the things that *Trout Fishing in America*—not just these three chapters—repeatedly suggests is that even in the trivial things of day-to-day American life there is a greater capacity for repression and authority than many of us would like to see. One of the finest political aspects of the novel is in fact Brautigan's ability to reveal such undercurrents even in incidents that might otherwise seem totally unremarkable or merely amusing.

Trout Fishing in America creates its own structure; it is the sort of organic text—its form developed naturally from the nature of its materials rather than from preconceived notions about what a novel *should* look like—that might please American theorists on literature from Ralph Waldo Emerson to Harold Bloom. But there is at least one outstanding American predecessor for the general, if not specific, form of the novel, and that is D. W. Griffith's film *Intolerance*. In that film, Griffith interlocks four stories from four historical epochs. All involve "intolerance," which, after all, is where Brautigan's own special concern, political and social repression, begins.

But what especially seems to link the novel and the film is Griffith's use of metaphor as a device to link his four stories. Intercut between episodes from the different stories are shots of a woman, played by Lillian Gish, rocking a cradle. These shots are accompanied by a subtitle borrowed from Whitman, "Out of the cradle endlessly rock-ing," the first line of his poem of the same name. The image serves Griffith, much as it originally served Whitman, to suggest an endless repetition in life, according to Griffith, of intolerance, destruction, and sorrow.

Considering Brautigan's own concern with history as essentially endless repetition (the conclusion, it will be remembered, of *A Confederate General from Big Sur*), it should not surprise us that he could be attracted to Griffith's film. Brautigan is also an avid filmgoer, and we have seen how *A Confederate General from Big Sur* reflects that interest. It should not surprise us then to find a model or suggestion for *Trout Fishing in America* in a film widely acknowledged to be the major achievement of silent films in America.

But one could also argue that there is a predecessor for the form of *Trout Fishing in America*, if not in American novels, then in American poetry. Whitman, after all, in "Song of Myself" utilized a central metaphor as the link between various sections of the poem. He was not, it is true, linking various narrative strands and so *Intolerance* seems closer to Brautigan's book and suggests itself more forcefully as the model, but the possibility of Whitman's influence should not be disregarded—not least because Griffith himself was clearly influenced by Whitman. At the least, shared interests make a line of influence from Whitman to Griffith to Brautigan possible.

Metaphor Is Its Own Reason

Aside from narrative and thematic links, *Trout Fishing in America* is clearly bound together by its central metaphor—like Griffith's cradle and Whitman's leaves of grass—which allows a vast variety of things—literature, folklore, politics, travel, and so forth—to be seen in close conjunction with each other rather than in the disparate way we usually view them. The result is a sense of America divided into two distinct but complementary "nations."

There is, first, the America of Lewis and Clark—a nation of frontiers and wilderness, great expectations and innocence, a paradise of wild and pastoral spendors. And then there is the America of big business and Hollywood, also an America of great expectations and innocence, but this time carefully calculated, designed by people in search of a profit, and up for sale. This is not the America of manifest destiny but the America, to cite the novel's example, of Deanna Durbin, that precocious child star of the 1930s who, with Shirley Temple, Judy Garland, and Mickey Rooney, helped Hollywood celebrate and sell youthful optimism and innocence during what was, up until then, unquestionably the bleakest decade in the nation's history. When an impoverished man can be sold optimism and innocence, he can be sold just about anything. Hollywood's America had little of the pastoral calm and none of the vast promise of the America of Lewis and Clark, but the optimism that characterized the earlier epoch had not yet vanished; it just had a new home—the movies.

Lewis and Clark's America is at home in schoolbooks and legend, and the America of Hollywood's fuzzy intelligence and values is the America which the narrator of *Trout Fishing in America* knew as a child. Both Americas have passed into history, but they continue to intrude on our lives and shape the way we think. In the novel's present— apparently 1960, although this can be guessed at only through a few vague political references—Americans, shaped by the past, are still optimistically fishing for something—but with diminished expecta- tions. The streams are polluted; the landscape, Thoreau to the contrary, can be and has been sold along with the land; and the closest that the narrator can get to nature, on the rainy February afternoon with which the book begins, is a small and not very interesting park in San Francisco. In the park, however, is a statue of Benjamin Franklin, which serves to remind us of that time when America was new and men fished for fortunes. The only fishing of any sort done in the park now is done by derelicts waiting and hoping for handouts, but the novel's point is that the "fishing" itself goes on, and so the past intrudes on the present.

The earlier Americas that the book shows us exist now in the political and mythic resonance of metaphors and images. That resonance is not logically demonstrated; it is asserted and felt in the various linkings of things with Trout Fishing in America. The book does not set out to prove that the past influences the present; it makes this fact felt in metaphor after metaphor. Lewis and Clark went trout fishing, and the narrator does it today. In effect, "Trout Fishing in America" is used, like the martial metaphors in *A Confederate General from Big Sur,* to suggest that the past perpetuates itself in the, or a, present. The present is not "new"; it is a repetition, in a sense, of the past, and America's present, alas, is merely the replay of a past, or rather of two pasts, that ideally would, but cannot, be relegated to history books.

Brautigan's vision emphasizes a commonplace and bleakly pessimistic view that America, sooner or later, transforms even its finest things into salable commodities.[7] It was a view adopted by the Beat movement, and while Brautigan certainly did not have to join the beats in San Francisco in order to find it, it was certainly to be found there together with many other assumptions about America that made their way into his novel. It would be helpful, for a moment, to look again at this literary movement of which Brautigan, as a latecomer, was associated.

City Lights

In 1960–61 when *Trout Fishing in America* was written, Brautigan was twenty-six and living on Greenwich Street in the North Beach section of San Francisco. This had been, a short while earlier, the center of the Beat movement, and anyone who spent much time in nearby coffee houses and bookstores would have seen, sooner or later, most of the important literary figures in the movement, including Allen Ginsberg, Gary Snyder, Jack Kerouac, Lawrence Ferlinghetti, Michael McClure, Philip Whalen, and others. Brautigan, as we have seen, was friendly with McClure and shared quarters with Whalen, a fellow Northwesterner and mystic poet and good friend of Snyder's. A regular among those who gathered at Ferlinghetti's City Lights bookstore, Brautigan, although somewhat younger than many of the most famous literary beats, knew and was well known to many of them.

But by the time *Trout Fishing in America* was written, many of the best-known beats were on their ways to new geographic and literary explorations. Snyder was in Japan studying Zen, and Ginsberg had temporarily deserted America for northern Africa and then the Orient and its religions. Kerouac remained behind, but most of his best writing had already been done, and in a short while he would be writing little at all. The Beat movement was rapidly dying, but the younger brother, so to speak, the last of the generation (rather than, as some would later argue, the first of the hippies), stayed to record one final time the Beat vision of America.

Like the beats, Brautigan remembered, and was deeply affected by, the Depression and the Second World War. If the subsequent years had produced only the Eisenhower presidency and the Korean war and Levittown, it had also provided that conservative, complacent consensus—conformist America—against which one could act out an individual rebellion for which James Dean, Marlon Brando, Little Richard, Kerouac, and others provided models. This kind of rebellion was very different from the collective social, often Marxist, rebellion of the 1930s or the equally collective rebellion of the New Left in the 1960s. The political extremists of the 1930s had been able to do little to direct America away from middle-class values, the alleged source of America's social and economic inequalities; to the rebel of the 1950s, rebellion was a personal matter. A man did not change the system; he changed himself. Kerouac's *On the Road* and Ginsberg's *Howl* are personal, idiosyncratic responses to a world that had, despite evident economic improvement, moved from an age of monumental despair to an age of monumental conformity. What the beats shared was their individual horror at what the nation, in the name of economic progress, had done to itself.

Much Beat literature mingles passionate affection and violent contempt for America. Ginsberg's early poetry, absorbing Whitman's politics along with his poetics, rages against an America that makes possible so much good that, as Whitman's *Democratic Vistas* made plain, it also destroys. Kerouac, Ferlinghetti, Ginsberg, Gregory Corso, and others repeatedly returned to personal visions of America as violent or, what could be worse, merely bland. But each man spoke for himself, and what makes their best works compelling is the sense of individuals speaking for themselves, testifying for themselves, not for some collective, adopted dogma.

The beats did not, despite their frequent lapses into polemic, primarily set out to change the world; they set out to change themselves, to reach beyond the limits and repressions of America, and to find an ecstatic personal awareness through whatever means promised fulfillment—mysticism, drugs, sex, and, especially in Kerouac, restless and relentless motion, forever searching for answers "on the road," continually reaching out, that is, for something beyond America's metaphysical boundaries. If anyone, to borrow Brautigan's metaphor, was fishing, and fishing desperately, for answers, it was the beats.

The beats' despair at what America had become was as fashionable among academics as it was among poets, but with this difference: that while universities were developing departments of social science to explore, understand, and (ideally) eradicate the problems—in, of course, rational, optimistic fashion—the beats acted as if the only solutions, at least the only ones that could be realized fully, were personal. You might rail at the enemy, but you could only reform yourself.

We have to start at this point, with this perspective on rebellion and America, if we are to understand *Trout Fishing in America.* Its picture of America as oppressive and morally weak was commonplace among the beats, but it was commonplace in a good many other quarters as well. But it is important to note that, like the beats, Brautigan can offer no collective or group solutions, only personal ones. It is an approach that would have been well understood in North Beach.

But he is quite unlike the beats in other ways. In particular, there is no rage or horror—like that in Ginsberg's *Howl*—at what America had become. He does not share the rational concern of the political liberal or the social scientist, the rage of the Beat writer, or the practiced ironic disengagement of the hipster. There is in fact almost a kind of contentment, but neither a smug nor an approving contentment, with America as it is. Brautigan's narrator is neither a reformer nor a prophet. He knows very well what is wrong with America but has neither the ambition nor the means to change it or even to escape from it.

And he has good reason for his calm in the midst of this political storm. Anger and rational solutions are both at this point irrelevant, for America, as understood by the narrator, is dying. The book is filled with references to death, and the report on Trout Fishing in America's autopsy is not entirely a joke.

Brautigan's narrator is simply aware of, not resigned to, nor even horrified by, what is happening to America. There is no cause now for

Kerouac's ceaseless wanderings or for drugs or for revolutions. The muddy political current of Beat literature has become a clear stream. There is really nothing to do now but sit back and watch.

Realpolitik

Beat literature, when not, as in Gary Snyder's poetry, dealing explicitly with nature or traditional Eastern or Amerindian myths, tended, directly or indirectly, to take America as its subject. In particular, this literature at times tended to conceptualize America as a vast manipulative bureaucracy conspiring against everything that makes men human. In place of humanity, this bureaucracy had erected its gods of money and materialism—metaphysical steamrollers crushing anything that did not enhance their authority. The first section of *Howl* is a catalog of the crimes which this system or bureaucracy had committed against those whom Ginsberg calls "the best minds of my generation." His rage at America is like that in the poetry of Corso and particularly Ferlinghetti, whose *Coney Island of the Mind* pictures the Americans with their automobiles, billboards, and freeways as "maimed citizens," occupying a Goyaesque hell.[8]

But the beats, after all, needed their sense of an insensitive, bureaucratic America against which to measure and justify their actions. There is a peculiar symbiotic relationship, a necessary but unhappy marriage between the two; and the one oddly complements the other.

It is, of course, the American present which offended the beats and which simultaneously provided the cause and justification for their literature. The past, in their view, had been betrayed, and indeed, among them, there was a persistent affection for, and identification with, nineteenth-century America. One of the happier, virtually sentimental aspects of *On the Road* is Kerouac's discovery of the survival of the past here and there throughout America—above all, his discovery of a gentle pastoralism among the Mexican-Americans of southern California. The beats' respect for the past can be found even in their aesthetics, their willingness to push aside much of the poetic experimentation and theory of the twentieth century in order to return to the innovations of Walt Whitman. Even their great respect for William

Carlos Williams fits this model, since Williams was very much a nineteenth-century man, both as a poet with clear allegiance to Whitman's prosody and professionally and privately as a small-town family doctor.[9]

The Cabinet of Doctor Caligari

The beats' sense of an ideal American past is to be found throughout *Trout Fishing in America.* It is the America of Lewis and Clark, the America of youthful optimism and ambition. A good example of this is the chapter entitled "The Cabinet of Doctor Caligari." The title is borrowed from the German expressionist film about a somnambulist who will do anything that his master, Caligari, wills him to do. The somnambulist is a sideshow exhibit, kept much of the time in a casket or "cabinet" but displayed from time to time for the amusement of incredulous crowds. Brautigan's chapter, like Caligari's cabinet, is a repository for sleepwalkers, two of them in fact: John Steinbeck and Henry David Thoreau. The first half of the chapter evokes memories of *Walden*; the second half, memories of *The Grapes of Wrath.* Steinbeck, Thoreau, and their books are never mentioned, but there can be no doubt that it is to them that Brautigan is referring.

Instead of a Massachusetts pond, the narrator studies mudpuddles in the Pacific Northwest. He is especially interested in water-bugs. He gets right down, looks closely into a mudpuddle, and discovers that the water-bugs have newspapers and playing-cards. One, he finds, has a harmonica. In the process, he is doing what Thoreau would do—study nature closely—and discovering something rather like what Thoreau discovered. In "Economy," the first chapter of *Walden,* Thoreau discusses formal education as shallow and misleading; he condemns "education" that teaches a man "to survey the world through a telescope or a microscope, and never with his naked eye."[10] Later in "Brute Neighbors," Thoreau takes his own advice and studies his woodpile, where he finds a battle between red ants and black ants, a Trojan war in miniature. Water-bugs are apparently more civilized.

Thoreau devoted a chapter of *Walden* to the value of reading and tells us of the importance to him, at Walden, of classical literature. It may be to this that Brautigan's narrator responds by selecting, for his progress into nature, "a pair of Sears Roebuck boots, ones with green rubber pages" (51).

At the end of his book, Thoreau tells us that he "left the woods for as good a reason as I went there. Perhaps it seemed to me that I had several more lives to live, and could not spare any more time for that one."[11] Brautigan's narrator, in accord, it may be, with our more pragmatic century, does not leave his mudpuddle only because he has other lives to live. He has no choice: the puddle dries up.

Brautigan is gently parodying Thoreau, but he is also making the point that Thoreau really has little to do with our world, our America, today; his pond has become our mudpuddle. Like Caligari's somnambulist, Thoreau of Walden is now a sleepwalker, brought out to amuse crowds in a world to which he no longer belongs and to which he can no longer both speak and expect to be understood. Thoreau, each time *Walden* is read, repeats himself; he goes through all the motions that he went through when the book was read for the first time. But perhaps in keeping with this mechanical age, his gestures are mechanical now— they are without human application, for the world he talks about is a world we have lost.

And so the narrator moves into the twentieth century, the world of the 1930s that seems now as much the province of a sleepwalker as the nineteenth century. He enters the world of *The Grapes of Wrath* where Okies are picking cherries for two and a half cents a pound, a world in which a man is either a faceless laborer or, if he is lucky, a celebrity. The celebrity here is Charles "Pretty Boy" Floyd, who was responsible for ten murders and more than thirty bank robberies, but whom the Okies worshiped as a hero, since he alone seemed to have found the way to beat the system.

There are many references to Floyd in *The Grapes of Wrath.* Typical is Ma Joad's reminiscence: "I knowed Purty Boy Floyd. I knowed his ma. They was good folks. He was full a hell, sure, like a good boy oughta be."[12] Her words tell us little about Floyd, but the point is that celebrities do not have to be characterized; they lend us a certain glory just by being in our presence. Their importance lies not in what they are as people but in what they represent. In similar fashion, one of the Okies in Brautigan's book, Rebel Smith, tells us that she was one of

Floyd's friends, but elaborating on this, all that she says is that she remembers running out onto her porch one day when Floyd drove up to her house (51). But, of course, she has gained the same thing that Ma Joad gained: a kind of honor and celebrity by association.

The Okies in *The Grapes of Wrath* are given an epic identity; Tom Joad is an Everyman, and Ma Joad fills the mythic role of the nurturing mother, source of all life, goodness, and growth. But these attributions are Steinbeck's, and in a crowd of actual people, the Joads would not, we feel, be exceptional; the characteristics which distinguish them are extraordinary perseverance and endurance, but in the day-to-day world, these would not make them seem epic. These people are, on the whole, anonymous, indistinguishable, and unexceptional. Brautigan's Okies are like Steinbeck's—without, however, the mythic associations. They are truly common men. Among the migrants working in the cherry orchards are some tramps, and, as the narrator pointedly says, "sometimes they [have] different faces" (52)—that is all that distinguishes one from another.

Trout Fishing in America suggests that common men, contrary to Steinbeck, are only common. There is no heroism, no epic presence here. And now we do not believe in the world of *The Grapes of Wrath* any more than we believe in *Walden*. Steinbeck and Thoreau belong to Americas very different from ours and so in a sense are sleepwalkers, mindlessly repeating their lessons, in our civilization today.

Another Millstone

Thoreau and Steinbeck respectively fit the two American pasts that, as we indicated earlier, underlie much of *Trout Fishing in America*—the earlier pastoral version and the later commercial one sponsored by Hollywood. It is worth noting in this respect that far more Americans knew Tom and Ma Joad through the film version in which they were portrayed by Henry Fonda and Jane Darwell than ever knew them through the book. The major difference between the book and the film lies in the film's greater glorification of the common man, and it is in this aspect of *The Grapes of Wrath* on which Brautigan focuses.

The book is replete with parodies (a fact overlooked by most of its critics), some evoking the high idealism of the nineteenth century, others evoking the literary and, more often, cinematic idealism of the 1930s. Among the latter is a fine parody of Ernest Hemingway's *For Whom the Bell Tolls* with a surrealistic twist that we would more likely have expected from William S. Burroughs. As with the parodies of Steinbeck and Thoreau, this parody implies that literature, like history, can betray us, leading us to believe things that are simply not true, at least in our world today. Perhaps there was a time when Hemingway's fiction convinced, but now it, too, is a sleepwalker, a hollow man, or a marionette, diverting us but, however charmingly, telling us little that is of practical use now. The poignance of the Hemingway idiom—insistingly aware, like Brett in *The Sun Also Rises,* of what might have been—serves nothing but sentimental ends.

In the Hemingway parody, which occurs in the chapter "Sea, Sea Rider," the owner of a bookstore asks the narrator if he would like to have sex—an unexpected question even in the narrator's San Francisco. As if he were in a Hemingway novel, the narrator responds with cool assurance, just as he might were he asked questions of this sort all the time, that no, he would rather not. But the owner persists, finds him a girl, and the narrator obediently has sex while the girl's boyfriend looks on. Both the girl and her boyfriend are as uninterested in, but as dutifully workmanlike about, the proceedings as is the narrator. Nor is anyone especially pleased by what is going on; each is simply doing what he has been asked to do. Certainly the stoic reserve of Hemingway heroes—grace under pressure—could not be more thoroughly, if ridiculously, parodied.

Only a typical Hemingway context has to be added, and that is what the bookstore owner proceeds to do. The narrator, he says, was a Communist; the girl was a painter. "When Barcelona fell, you and she flew to England, and then took ship back to New York. Your love for each other remained in Spain. It was only a war love" (25). And then the parody moves to further extremes. The scene shifts to Mexico, a thirteen-year-old girl, and scandalous goings-on, in which Brautigan's narrator expresses neither surprise nor interest. The owner concludes his story by saying that neither the narrator nor his girl friend "lived to be twenty-one. It was not necessary" (26). And so the narrator, finally free of unwanted demands on himself, returns to his book. If anything significant has happened, it is solely in the bookstore owner's imagination. For everyone else, Hemingway and high romance are just two of life's little interruptions.

The Spanish Civil War is, of course, a legacy of the 1930s, but it was not a cause that inspired great American interest—until, that is, Hemingway published his novel and Hollywood released the film version starring Gary Cooper. Certainly more people, as we would expect, saw the film than read the book, and so as with *The Grapes of Wrath*, a Hollywood-sponsored product provided the official version of our past.

Slogans and Labels

Trout Fishing in America is, among other things, a compilation of the things that have become America and that America has become. The book refers to a vast variety of places, people, and things from American history, literature, politics, and popular culture: Richard Nixon, Henry Wadsworth Longfellow, Henry Miller, William S. Burroughs, John Dillinger, Ed Sullivan, Caryl Chessman, Chubby Checker, Charles "Pretty Boy" Floyd, Andrew Carnegie, the Andrews Sisters, Beatniks, the Zoot Suit, Mormons, Woolworth's, Nelson Algren, Metrical, Meriwether Lewis, "Sea, Sea Rider" (C. C. Rider), the Twist, and Kool-Aid are all mentioned. So are Tacoma, Salt Lake City, New York, Pittsburgh, New Orleans, Cleveland, Fort Lauderdale, San Francisco, Los Angeles, Missoula (Montana), and Mooresville (Indiana).

But the book is especially rich in references to, and parodies of, literary works. *Trout Fishing in America* is a highly literate and literary book, but it does not limit itself to "serious" literary concerns. It also records signs and slogans with which America has documented its presence across the landscape—signs and slogans that may comprise the only American "literature" that many Americans ever know. The signs include an inscription on a monument dedicated to the Civilian Conservation Corps and an inscription to the memory of three men killed in an airplane crash while searching for survivors of an earlier crash. The book also reproduces an FBI poster, a no-trespassing sign, and a sign warning that cyanide capsules have been spread around the area to kill coyotes—although, of course, there is the possibility, perhaps even the likelihood, that some unfortunate people may discover the capsules before they discover the sign.

The signs all suggest that something is (or was) wrong or should be (or should have been) avoided. A man named Alonso Hagen, who, in seven years of fishing expeditions, has caught nothing, summarizes his experience by calling it "an interesting experiment in total loss" (85). Most of the slogans and signs, like the literary parodies, add up to a sense of total loss or at least its possibility. America's signs and slogans, at least those recorded in the novel, promise little or nothing that most people would want to find.

At one point, for example, the narrator comes across a tombstone for a man named John Talbot who was killed—or, precisely, "Had His Ass Shot Off / In a Honky-Tonk"—in 1936, when he was eighteen. The inscription goes on to say that his sister left wilted flowers in the mayonnaise jar at the grave and that she "Is In / The Crazy Place Now" (21). According to Brautigan, the inscription echoes one in *Moby-Dick* to another John Talbot, who died a hundred years earlier, also at the age of eighteen.[13] This John Talbot, whose monument, according to the inscription, was erected by his sister, "was lost overboard, / Near the Isle of Desolation, off Patagonia."[14] The heroic John Talbot of the nineteenth century has been exchanged for the silly, comic Talbot of the twentieth, and the sister who, as would have then been said, "had lost her mind with grief," has been exchanged for one who has simply lost her mind. The twentieth century, it seems, has no room for sentiment or heroism. There is indeed no heroism or sentiment at all in the present portrayed by *Trout Fishing in America*; in these respects at least, it depicts a "total loss" culture.

In the chapter immediately following that in which the narrator records the modern John Talbot inscription, he tells us that he went into a bookstore and came across a book about Billy the Kid. There is no further reference to this fact, but we are apparently supposed to compare that nineteenth-century hero—or villain—with Talbot. Billy the Kid, after all, died the same way Talbot did, but half a century earlier, and when it happened, it became no joke but part of American history and legend.

The inscriptions collected in the book, like the various parodies, consistently and repeatedly suggest that the American past and its literature—whether by literature we mean *Walden* or epitaphs—have little to do with the way we live now. Our "literatures" today—as suggested by the signs and slogans that mark our landscape—have nothing heroic or desirable in them; the good qualities are in the past. It is, therefore, no surprise when the narrator, telling us about a bookstore in which he likes to browse, says that it is "a parking lot for used graveyards" (22).

Fishing in Time

If Brautigan had wished to open his novel with an inscription from the American past, he would have done well to take the following from *Walden*: "Time is but the stream I go a-fishing in. I drink at it; but while I drink I see the sandy bottom and detect how shallow it is. Its thin current slides away, but eternity remains. I would drink deeper; fish in the sky, whose bottom is pebbly with stars."[15] Brautigan's narrator has also fished in time—or time's written record—and he also has found it shallow, the repository of dead, unusable pasts (which, paradoxically, include *Walden*). Like Thoreau, as we will later see, he would fish in the sky, eternity, but the present moment ties him down, much as it would have tied down Lee Mellon and his friends had they not escaped to Big Sur.

The chapters that deal specifically with the narrator's fishing expeditions complete the impression of an America currently permeated by death and decay. "Red Lip," the chapter with which the account of these expeditions begins, mentions "an old abandoned shack that had a sheriff's notice [a no-trespassing sign!] nailed like a funeral wreath to the front door" (6), and the chapters that follow are replete with a byzantine maze of references to, and metaphors involving, death, abandonment, and legal and other prohibitions. Indeed the sequence of chapters that deals with the expeditions ends with the narrator and his friends abandoning the countryside and returning (we assume, although he does not say this explicitly) to San Francisco. Before they return, they find, in back of an abandoned home, an old outhouse, and they use it to store their garbage until—like the American past and the American landscape that they are deserting—it is full almost to overflowing with stuff that nobody needs anymore.

The narrator's fishing trip—the actual trip as well as his fishing through through the American past—has been, like Alonso Hagen's, an "experiment in total loss" (83). More often than not (or so it seems), the trout are dead before the narrator arrives to catch them—or have swum away long ago. In one episode, someone tries to stock a trout stream only to have the fish die as soon as they are put in the water. In another stream, the narrator and his female companion make love in the water surrounded by green slime and dead fish, one of which—"His eyes . . . stiff like iron"—floats down into the white string of the narrator's sperm (44).

Even when things are pleasant, they are not pleasant for long. At one point, the narrator catches a pretty little trout, but all around him are cyanide capsules to kill coyotes, and soon he finds he can only think about a gas chamber. Whatever pleasure he might have had in his catch has been thoroughly contaminated.

Happy in America

The America that *Trout Fishing in America* describes should be no one's paradise, but Americans paradoxically remain optimistic that if they do not now have what they want, they eventually will. The first chapter describes a San Francisco park with the statue of Benjamin Franklin pictured on the cover of the novel. Franklin, first among American businessmen, was also first among American optimists; he always had faith in the future. Gathered around the statue are derelicts looking for a free handout, and we are assured that they will eventually get what they want. Derelicts and Franklin are alike at least in their optimism, and the chapter ends with a quotation from Franz Kafka: "I like the Americans because they are healthy and optimistic" (2).

Even those who have reason to conclude that America is a total loss do not entirely give up hope—as witness the derelicts in hope of a handout. Alonso Hagen in fact is the only man, except the narrator, who would even suggest that he has reached the end of the road, that he is faced with total loss. One of the narrator's friends, for example, having run out of money and with no other acceptable alternatives for the future, decides to spend the coming winter in an asylum, where he will have everything from television to locked razors to pretty nurses. "No winter spent there," he concludes, "could be a total loss" (18).

In Brautigan's America, there is always, somewhere, something to ward off the evident conclusion that it is optimism itself that prevents us from seeing the total loss that lies around us. In an asylum with locked razors, despair is beside the point; if optimism can make even the asylum look good, there is not much left to do except laugh—and *Trout Fishing in America* has some very funny chapters.

Rebellion

Healthy, optimistic America with its endless prohibitions, laws, and signs of decay and death was, as we said, the America against which beats and others rebelled in the 1950s. Without this America, one could no more have had the films of Marlon Brando and James Dean or the music of Little Richard and Elvis Presley than one could have had *Howl, On the Road, Naked Lunch,* or *Trout Fishing in America.* However valid or false this America may historically be—and there are those who would argue that the comparative economic and political stability of the decade made it a good time to be around—it was this America that provided the foil for the disenchantment, anger, restlessness, and rebellion that is found throughout so much that is good in the popular literature, film, and music of the time.

Many of the political matters to which the book refers—the Kennedy-Nixon campaign, the "Communist conspiracy," and so forth—are as dated as handouts from the Berkeley Free Speech Movement and, for that matter, were in the late 1960s and early 1970s when the book was most popular. But while *The Wild One* and *Rebel Without a Cause* seem hopelessly dated today, Brautigan's novel, together with much that is best among the writings of the Beat generation, remains powerful and convincing.

The explanation for this lies not so much in Brautigan's selection of historical facts and incidents to document his impression of America as in the way the narrator presents them, for while the subject matter has definite historical specificity and so would be expected to date quickly, the narrator's voice is not tied to the time and place he describes. The historical details of *Rebel Without a Cause* date the film absolutely, and no one can watch it now with the same intensity of identification that audiences in the 1950s did. (No one, for example, drives the kind of car that James Dean does or even acts quite the way he does. The gestures belong in subtle ways to a particular time.) *Trout Fishing in America* is a very different kind of enterprise, however. The narrator may not be like us or even like anyone we know, yet at the same time, there is little about him—as opposed to the America he describes—which is specifically of the 1950s.

Time is the stream that he, like Thoreau, goes fishing in, but he stands on the bank and is never swept away by the current. Like Jesse in *A Confederate General from Big Sur,* he is profoundly aware of history and time, yet he is placid, passive in the face of what he discovers; he testifies to what he finds, and we believe in him implicitly.

It is in the creation of this narrator that much of Brautigan's achievement in this novel lies, and understanding the nature of, and necessity for, this narrator is a complex matter, best set off in a chapter by itself.

Chapter Four

The Center of the Earth

Personal Solutions

Tom Robbins's novel *Still Life with Woodpecker* (1980) summarizes a political position which the narrator of *Trout Fishing in America* would surely have understood: ". . . no matter how fervently a romantic might support a [political] movement," writes Robbins, attributing the ideas to "learned professors" at Outlaw College,

> he or she must eventually withdraw from active participation in the move-
> ment because the group movement—the supremacy of the organization over
> the individual—is an affront to intimacy. Intimacy is the principal source
> with which this life is sweetened.[1]

This romantic does not want to limit himself, to surrender his freedom to anyone or any group. He is in search of "the power of higher consciousness, which, while universal, cosmic even, is manifest in the intimate."[2]

Robbins is a comic novelist, equal to, but far more bizarre and flamboyant than, Donald Barthelme, Kurt Vonnegut, or Philip Roth, and there is little that he touches that he cannot turn to humor. Nonetheless, there is no joke in the above quotation; he is quite serious, as the rest of the novel makes plain.

Robbins's romantic sides with the uncompromising libertarianism of the hipster or beatnik rather than with the communal politics of the New Left and the counterculture in general. Robbins's statements are, in fact, a fine summary of a political position found in works by such men as Ginsberg, Kerouac, and Brautigan. At issue here is the assumption that collective enterprises, no matter how good or well meaning they may be, eventually corrupt their followers. A man may sympathize with the principles shared by a group, but no more than

Thoreau at Walden should he identify directly with any group or consistently, actively, and publicly support it.

And this is the political ground on which the narrator of *Trout Fishing in America* stands. He shares with a great many of his time an awareness of what America has done to itself, but the political things that he writes about—peace marches and an anti-HUAC demonstration, for example—interest him as an outsider. He mentions a peace march which *"they"* (his italics) have organized, but he does not join it (98). The narrator is simply not interested *personally* in politics; it is just another aspect of America worth watching.

Politically, he simply does not give a damn, and it is in part because of this that we are so easily seduced into believing that his political image of America is accurate. Why would he lie when, as his every word and action testify, he does not personally care—when, that is, all he does is "fish" and tell us, objectively, about his catch? The man whom we are most likely to trust is the one who is a good, objective reporter but who has no personal stake in what he reports.

But devising a book in which we are deeply interested in what, after all, is a disengaged, indifferent voice, reporting on things long past, is no small achievement. American narrators like Ishmael and Huck Finn are personally involved with their subjects. We may have to distinguish between the way things are and the way they are reported, yet, despite our hesitation at fully accepting as fact everything that the narrator tells us, we are in great measure seduced into the narrative by the personal intensity with which the story is told. We care about the narrative because the narrator does, and we care about him.

Brautigan's narrator, on the other hand, is too passive to be a participant. Things happen to him, and he sees things happen, and he reports his information without the sense that he was in a meaningful way effected. Since he is largely indifferent to what he finds and since he only reports and is not substantially altered by his experiences, he presents special problems both for his creator and for his critics. In the solution of these problem lies, however, the cause and explanation for much of the narrative power that makes *Trout Fishing in America* such an exceptional book.

Inward Journey

Raymond M. Olderman in a study of contemporary American literature argued that there were "almost no journeys in the novels of the sixties. . . . a massive static institution or background [had] taken the place of the journey as a symbol for the obstacles of human experience."[3]

Trout Fishing in America is, of course, in part about a journey, but the book conveys little sense of *progress* from place to place and repeatedly suggests that, aside from details of landscape, one place in America is very much like another. In Brautigan's America, there is not much reason to travel, for what there is to find we have found and know already. This is exactly what we would expect from the author of *A Confederate General from Big Sur,* denying, as it does, the idea of progress and insisting that all possibilities may be, at any given moment, present. This conclusion, within the context of the novel, is positive, for it suggests that men like Jesse can be exactly what they, not the times in which they live, think they should be; he need not be limited by history. History or at least its concurrent idea of progress through time is an illusion—or so the novel suggests.

But as soon as this idea is applied to the public world rather than the self, it invites a kind of fatalism. If things do not progress, people can do nothing to alter *permanently* the way things are, and there is no reason to believe that things will, of their own accord, change for the better.

In the previous chapter, we argued that the world of the novel is not an objective record of things as they are, or were but simply a version, and a subjective one at that, which Brautigan shared with many other Beat writers. In any case, it is the fundamental assumption of the book that the narrator merely reports what is; there is never a suggestion that he tampers with evidence in order to make it fit his political preconceptions.

There is, therefore, a sense of inevitability throughout the novel. The narrator tells us what is, and there is nothing that can be done to change it. The idea of a journey, with its attendant suggestions of growth and progress, is illusory.

Where Do We Go From Here?

In the next to the last chapter of *Trout Fishing in America*, the narrator quotes an anthropologist to the effect that no one can start a new culture; he's stuck, that is, with what he's got. Lee Mellon may withdraw into his imaginary world, but unless we do the same, the rest of us had better be resigned to what we've got. That at least is the implication of the novel.

Nor is the situation lightened by traditional values. There is no sense in the novel that fulfilling obligations, for example, would make the situation palatable; the narrator is a husband and a father, but neither of these roles or obligations seems to bring him any satisfaction.

The people in the novel who can be considered survivors—men, that is, who are not victimized by their society—are men like "Pard," never willing to settle down into conventional life and willing to try just about anything (as long as it is not conventional) at least once. He has lived in Idaho, Paris, San Francisco, and Arizona. He has worked for newspapers, and he has worked on a tugboat. He has studied existentialism and is now reading Genet, Burroughs, and Krafft-Ebing. Currently he works as a type-setter specializing in avant-garde work. He is always collecting new experiences—new ideas, new places, new jobs. People like Pard survive by never settling down; they are never in one place long enough to have it affect them in any deep or lasting way.

Men like Pard depend utterly on themselves. They are also moral, intellectual, and emotional travellers. Even if they were forced to stay in one place, they would, we assume, always be looking for new things to understand and enjoy.

Home Again

When the narrator returns from his last fishing expedition, he goes to Pard's cabin. Pard's way of life, his eclectic interests, and his refusal to settle down and to take things as they come are ways of surviving the America which the narrator has discovered. As long as a man never reaches a final point of rest, a commitment, he is potentially free of the demands which an unreasonable America can make. He can always move on.

Brautigan's novel is as eclectic and diverse as Pard's life; it is, as we have seen, a collection of names, incidents, and facts, all of which the narrator has encountered but none of which has held his interest for very long. Like Pard, he is always ready to move on. In effect, he tells us that only the traveling, only the perpetual seeking out of new experiences, is what matters. There is none of Pard's hyperexcitement, but there is perpetual seeking, nonetheless. Like the motorcyclist in Brautigan's "The Nature Poem," he has nothing to travel toward; it is the motion, the traveling itself, that counts.

It is worth comparing *Trout Fishing in America* in its richly eclectic diversity with Kerouac's *Visions of Cody,* which in style and substance comes as close as Kerouac ever came to his ideal of "spontaneous prose." The book is a collage of anecdotes and information about Neal Cassady, the real-life beat hero whose experiences were even more diverse and numerous than Pard's. Things in the book seldom occur in any special order except the order imposed by memory at the moment of composition. Parts of the book were "written" on a tape recorded by Kerouac and Cassady himself. Despite the fact that parts of the novel are wordy, diffuse, and repetitious, it has a tremendous cumulative power and intensity. Kerouac's intensity of consciousness—his uncompromising insistence on showing things exactly as they are rather than as they might appear after reflection or thought—gives the book its powerful central focus. Without it, the book would seem merely disorganized or chaotic.

Although Brautigan, as we have seen, owes much to Kerouac's "spontaneous prose," he never quite lets go the way Kerouac could, giving us long, convoluted, and intense sentences that show us things with all the excitement and immediacy that a forceful actor might be able to convey if he were speaking to us directly. Brautigan's sentences and observations, quieter and more passive than anything in Kerouac, may reflect an interest in Zen quietism. Kerouac is aggressively interested in finding and showing us new things, new experiences, but Brautigan is reserved, meditative, passively waiting for the experience to come to him. His perpetual seeking is metaphysical and emotionally withdrawn. The differences between the central metaphors in the best-known works by the two men are instructive; Kerouac is forever on the road, actively seeking things out; Brautigan has gone fishing, and he stands on the bank of the stream waiting for things to come to him.

An example from D. T. Suzuki's essay comparing Eastern and Western modes of thought may be helpful in explaining the special values of Brautigan's approach. Suzuki compares a poem by the Japanese writer Basho with Alfred, Lord Tennyson's "Flower in the Crannied Wall." Basho's haiku is simple and direct, noting a fact in nature—a flower in bloom by a hedge.

In Tennyson's poem, on the other hand, the poet plucks the flower and, addressing it, says,

> . . . if I could understand
> What you are, root and all, and all in all,
> I should know what God and man is.

As Suzuki points out, Basho is content to deal with his experience directly; it is an intuitive approach, one that involves an immediate apprehension of meaning. Tennyson, on the other hand, is objective, logical. Suzuki analyzes the differences between the two poems—and the very different kinds of intelligence that they imply—at considerable length and finds in these differences the great distinction between East and West.[4]

Brautigan's narrator is closer to Basho than Tennyson; the narrator is, like Basho, passive, aware, intuitively apprehending. In American literature, the narrative voice closest to the Eastern model is Whitman in *Leaves of Grass,* a voice supremely aware and certain but also intuitive and passive. Like Basho and Brautigan, Whitman sets out to change neither himself nor the world; he wishes to understand, not change; there is none of the aggressive intensity that we find, for example, in Kerouac.

We have already pointed out various similarities between Whitman's work and Brautigan's, and it may be that the narrative voice in *Trout Fishing in America* has origins in *Leaves of Grass,* but it is more likely, given Brautigan's particular interest in Zen culture, that the voice has its origins in Eastern attitudes. The very passivity and detachment of the narrative voice are far from the aggressive and rapturous voice that we find throughout much of *Leaves of Grass.*

Whatever the origins of the narrative voice in *Trout Fishing in America,* the effect is to make us deal with things directly, without analysis or interpretation. We see things head-on, as if for the first time. It is appropriate that the book begins with a photograph, for, above all, *Trout Fishing in America* tries to make us *see,* not interpret as language usually invites us to do (and as, alas, we are at this moment doing).

We began our discussion of the novel by pointing out its extraordinary *documentary* effect—the sense that we are dealing with a kind of personal witness or testimony, a record of things as they are. If, on the one hand, it is true that the America to which the narrator bears witness is largely one shared by Beat writers, among others, in the 1950s, it is equally true that this vision is conveyed with an unqualified honesty, utterly convincing.

The narrative voice and the type of awareness it implies—passive, meditative, honest—are in effect the book's solution for those who must survive in the America that is described for us. Like the narrator, we can stand on the banks of the river, where we passively wait, watch, and understand—but commit ourselves to nothing.

Brautigan's book derives in many ways from the 1950s, but it says much for the wisdom of the book's vision that it survives, not as a relic of another past like the past of pastoral America, irretrievably gone; for the vision itself, if not the facts and data it records, finally owes no allegiance to time. It can cut itself off from any historical moment and—like Pard, the book's ideal—go anywhere. With limits and restraints it ultimately has nothing to do.

Chapter Five

The Center of the Universe

A World of Sugar

In Watermelon Sugar, Brautigan's third novel, is his shortest but in some respects his most ambitious. Unlike *Trout Fishing in America* and *A Confederate General from Big Sur,* it deals with history and politics only indirectly and centers instead on the other characteristic concern of Brautigan's fiction, the self and its relation to the world of shared experience. It is also a very funny novel, delighting us in the cavalier, but completely honest, fashion in which it resolves complex problems with simple and obvious solutions. It is at the same time the most serious of Brautigan's three early novels, the one which most succinctly demonstrates a special narrative point of view shared with *A Confederate General from Big Sur* and *Trout Fishing in America.*

The narrator of *In Watermelon Sugar* is, in effect, the subject of the book; although he tells us many facts, he can tell us comparatively little about the character and personality of anyone except himself. He is, like other Brautigan narrators, confronted with a corrupt, violent world, and like them, he survives it morally uneffected. But while this survival is merely a *given* in *Trout Fishing in America* and little more than that in *A Confederate General from Big Sur, In Watermelon Sugar* shows explicitly how that survival is possible.

The novel was written between May and July 1964, and was published by the Four Seasons Foundation in 1968. It was soon, like earlier Brautigan novels, required reading in the counterculture, and it is not difficult to see why. The book is set in the future at a commune that, unlike many, actually works; people are truly content there. It is the sort of place that many in the counterculture tried, but failed, to establish.

In the book, much of civilization as we know it has been relegated to the "Forgotten Works." No one lives there, and by unwritten law, entrance to the Forgotten Works is forbidden. The good things in life—things which are gentle, pleasant, kind—flourish nearby in a small town that sounds like nothing so much as the sort of small American village that never existed outside such Hollywood films as the Hardy family series of the 1930s and 1940s.

There is a general store, a family doctor, a local "café" where the day's gossip is passed around. People travel by horse, not car, for this is a world without machines. Technology has been shut away with other evils in the Forgotten Works. Life is conducted in a leisurely fashion; there are few reasons to rush; endings are always happy.

Near the village, however, is something that would have been quite out of place in an Andy Hardy film; this is iDEATH, a commune where no one has to do more than he wants, but where everything (miraculously) seems to get done and get done right. Here things are made from "watermelon sugar," and since the sun shines a different color each day of the week and the watermelons take on the color of the sunlight, there are seven kinds of watermelon sugar—red, gold, gray, black, white, blue, and brown. iDEATH (despite its name) is the ideal place to live—aesthetically delightful and *never* threatening. Many of those who live here are as sugary as the watermelon sugar from which their world is built. They do not understand envy and hate. Competition is unknown.

At iDEATH, there is no history, no sense of a past except for vague memories of the time of the tigers, who spoke good English but hunted people down for food. But the time of the tigers has no significance in the present, and the present is what matters. When the narrator tells us about the past, it is, with few exceptions, because he dreams about it—and it is the dreams (a present of sorts), not the past itself, that he describes for us.

But in the midst of this gentle, pastoral calm, there once was a villain, a former member of the commune whose name was inBOIL and who gathered a group of disciples and began to explore the Forgotten Works. He decided—with the refreshing lack of subtlety that distinguishes everyone here—to lead a life of violence, and the violence led eventually to a ritual bloodbath in which he and his followers destroyed themselves.

One of the women at the commune, Margaret, was fascinated with inBOIL and his violence, and at the end of the book, she, following his example, commits suicide. The local community and the commune hold her funeral on a black day, a day without light or sound. At the end of the book, the funeral over, the mourners are waiting for the black day to end so that they can have a dance.

A dance? In this world, grief and sorrow, like the other unpleasant things in life, have been left behind at the Forgotten Works. Indeed, in this world, all extreme emotions—ecstasy and passion as well as grief—have been forgotten. The people here are so gentle that we would assume that they would be highly vulnerable; paradoxically, they are not vulnerable at all. As the narrator says of one of the commune's members, she "had a lot of strength gained through the process of gentleness" (21).[1] And he could have said the same thing of himself or of anyone else in the book—except, of course, anyone who ventured into the Forgotten Works.

Gentle People

In Watermelon Sugar is reminiscent of another futuristic utopia in which extreme emotions have been eliminated, B. F. Skinner's *Walden II*; passion and tragedy are as absent from Skinner's utopia as they are from Brautigan's, but the means through which this is achieved are very different. Skinner gets his utopia by imposing an intellectual system on people; he trains them to act only in ways he thinks are acceptable. In a sense this is what Brautigan does when he relegates all the unpleasant things to the Forgotten Works, but he does not stop there. Skinner is the objective, rational thinker who arranges his utopia from the outside. The people in his utopia are the puppets of a system. Brautigan, on the other hand, constructs his utopia the other way around. Although he readily clears the landscape of everything objectionable, collecting them and placing them in the Forgotten Works, his real interest is in the way his people perceive things rather than, like Skinner's, in the things they perceive. Skinner shows us a model of social efficiency; Brautigan takes us inside one of his utopians to acquaint us intimately with a utopian perspective or point of view.

In Watermelon Sugar suggests that the world is exactly what we make of it, and if we include suffering, guilt, passion, and grief, we may only have constructed prisons for ourselves.

The narrator of the book constructs no prisons for himself. It is a fundamental Buddhist assertion that the root of suffering lies in the endemic human belief in the phenomenal world and its pageant of perpetual change. Salvation begins when one frees oneself from that illusion, when one renounces the belief that phenomena are absolutely real. Consciously or not, the narrator of the book has made this renunciation. He is not emotionally touched by the phenomenal world except when it fortifies the gentle, passive self that he is.

Motion without Movement

Like *A Confederate General from Big Sur, In Watermelon Sugar* is partially concerned with showing that the appearance of change, namely that which we call history, is relative, by and large, to an individual's point of view. The appearance of historical change is a fiction to be resisted. Unlike most of us, the narrator is not concerned with the variety or progress of experience. He does not change; there is no sense of interaction between the individual and history—unless he trespasses into the Forgotten Works. At the end of the book, the narrator is the same person that he was at the beginning.

The narrator is like the Taoist or Buddhist absorbed in the ultimate paradox: a universe that appears to change but essentially does not change at all, being ultimately the great, ineffable void. Although our awareness of the narrator and his friends may change, it is not that they have become different people but that we simply know more about them.

It is true that *In Watermelon Sugar* contains a narrative or plot, but this narrative, such as it is, is *imposed* on the novel, and the narrator's consciousness, by inBOIL, his gang, and Margaret. But this is entirely their work; there is nothing inevitable about it. The narrator is without motive, and he is in no way altered by the story he tells us. Like the narrator of *Trout Fishing in America,* what he fundamentally does is witness and record but remain wholly uneffected by the story and information that he passes on to us. The novel's final image—the commune and community merely existing within a black, soundless day—suggests the way things are supposed to be: without motion or purpose except that provided naturally by the passing of time. (Time, incidentally, is not recorded—or created—by clocks or any other human device; people tell time by, they say, studying the rivers—by attending, that is, to nature rather than by creating artificial measurement.)

If there is, then, little or no historical change at iDEATH, there is a kind of natural change, which the narrator perceives but is apparently unable to do more than suggest to us. It appears to be a kind of change that transcends any rational or literal description and is suggested by repeated references to streams that flow through and characterize iDEATH—one in fact flows through the house—as compared with the forbidding mountains which are found at, and which characterize, the Forgotten Works. At the Forgotten Works, nature is static, unmoving—it is historical change that matters there; at iDEATH, on the other hand, there is perpetual natural change. To phrase it another way, change at iDEATH is without "events," without history. It is the sort of change that does not need laws or politics or any of the other paraphernalia of civilization in order to keep going.

Whatever Is, Is

"It suits us" and "It's for the best" are refrains repeated throughout the book, beginning with the first page. No matter what happens, it is, we are told, for the best; it is exactly what should be.

At iDEATH is a "statue of mirrors," which seems to serve, for Brautigan, a symbolic function that is difficult to penetrate and interpret. It seems to be iDEATH's one concession to history; in it, the people at the commune can see "events" that are occurring elsewhere, but they are unable to understand or interpret the purpose behind those events. Like the jar in Wallace Stevens's poem "The Anecdote of the Jar," it seems to possess all that it reflects. Looking into the "statue of mirrors" is like looking at the actual event; the statue does not interpret things—it shows them just as they are.

It is while looking at the statue that the narrator sees Margaret kill herself. He knows what is happening and where it is happening, but he does nothing to stop it. Indeed, he is so cut off from ordinary feelings that he can feel nothing toward what he sees. He cannot feel resignation or alarm or concern; he merely watches and records what he finds. But he does not understand it; it is an action tied to the Forgotten Works, and so all that he can do is to watch and tell us what he sees.

At the end of *A Confederate General from Big Sur,* Jesse is so high on dope (and his transcendent awareness of history) that he can do nothing but sit and watch things pass. It is this kind of awareness, totally abstracted from conventional concerns and from emotional involvement in anything that is not gentle and passive, that *In Watermelon Sugar* shows us.

Our sense of paradox thrives on the awareness of distinction, but at iDEATH, paradoxes cannot exist or, to put it another way, are instantly resolved. Distinctions—except, it may be, the distinctions between iDEATH and the Forgotten Works—are blurred or simply unknown. Jesse in *A Confederate General from Big Sur* has to learn to survive paradox and conflict, and he does so through his transcendent view of history and, of course, his alcohol and marijuana. The narrator of *In Watermelon Sugar,* however, has never learned what paradox and conflict are, and since he has never learned what they are, he never sees them.

iDEATH

iDEATH requires of its members that passive, unified, and certainly, to our way of thinking, narrow sense of experience which the narrator and his book demonstrate and which, in turn, they are. iDEATH is more than a place or group of people; it is exactly what its name suggests: the death of the "i" or ego or self. At one point, inBOIL claims that *he* is iDEATH, but that, obviously, is not true. He is, in fact, the very opposite: the ego turned in on itself, feeding on itself. For him, suicide, the violent destruction of the self, is a logical culmination to things, the true iDEATH.

Suicide would not, however, be possible for the narrator or the other inhabitants of the commune. The narrator is, in fact, what inBOIL claims to be: iDEATH; he has no self—or at least as little as he could have and still operate from day to day. All he can do is record things; there is not enough of a "self" and consequently not enough will to make things happen. He does stay away from Margaret, and he does write a book, but the former results from the fact that, having entered the Forbidden Works, she has little in common with him any more, and his book is far more the expression of a point of view than any expression of self. Writing the book, he makes clear, is merely something he does; there is no motivation, no purpose, no will behind it. Total death of the "i" or self would be impossible outside death itself—in that, at least, inBOIL knows what he is talking about—but the narrator comes about as close to that end as a person could and yet still live and interact at all meaningfully with others.

In keeping with this virtual lack of "self," the narrator has no name. "My name depends on you," he tells the reader. "Just call me whatever is in your mind" (4). Identity, if there is to be any, is the reader's problem, not his.

A final example of this point of view and its implications may be helpful. "The Statue of Mirrors," like the narrator and iDEATH, has no identity of its own; what it does is absorb and reflect the world around it, but it does not interpret things or give "meaning" to anything. We never see the statue itself; all that we can see is what it reflects, but the narrator insists that if we are to see those reflections, we must "empty [our minds] of everything else but the mirrors, and [we] must be careful not to want anything from the mirrors. They just have to happen" (112). If the statue is iDEATH's link to the world of events, it also suggests a state of total, undirected, undiscriminating awareness—the kind of awareness perhaps that, according to Buddhist and Taoist thought, allows us to perceive truly, without the justifications, explanations, and reasonings of history.

Last Rites

In this novel where the death of the self allows a man to enter a finer existence, death itself is now something to be celebrated. The people at iDEATH have elaborate burial rituals. What else could we expect where stillness, passivity, silence, and peace are the treasured values? iDEATH is made from death. So little actually happens here that the people have nothing to discuss but the most commonplace and trivial things. (It is appropriate that the narrator's only literary accomplishment before writing *In Watermelon Sugar* was an essay on the weather.) So little actually transpires that the local newspaper is published only once a year.

Much is made of the fact that the narrator is writing a book—the very book, of course, that we are reading. If there is not a need for a newspaper more than once a year, then what can the narrator find to write about? In fact, all that he can do is tell us what things at iDEATH are like and then record what he knows of the incidents involving inBOIL, his gang, and Margaret; in iDEATH itself, there is little to be said. Asked at one point what his book is about, he replies, "Just what I'm writing down: one word after another" (107).

The book ends with the narrator's saying, "The musicians were poised with their instruments. They were ready to go. It would only be a few seconds now, I wrote" (138). We know no more than he writes, and he writes only what he sees, even when he does not understand exactly the meaning—our conventional interpretation—of those things. Like Whitman in *Leaves of Grass,* the narrator of *Trout Fishing in America,* or the enlightened Buddhist, he is, in his passivity, utterly calm and honest. Thoroughly disinterested and detached from the confusions and expectations of our conventional world, he is able to see and record experience with an honesty that few of us could match.

And he has his reward, for if he experiences no great emotion and does not know the "meaning" of the events he reports, he is a genuinely contented man.

Full Circle

Among Brautigan's early novels, *In Watermelon Sugar* most deserved its reputation in the counterculture. It is true that the book, in its idiosyncratic point of view, seems to have more to do with the rampant individualism or philosophical anarchism that we associate with the Beat generation than with the communal attitudes of the counterculture, and, in fact, the narrator's associations with other members of iDEATH are as emotionless and cold as his associations with others, including inBOIL. But it is still a communal ethic that Brautigan outlines here, even if not a warm or necessarily inviting one, and that alone justified its reputation in the counterculture.

The book was not published until 1968, four years after it was written, but that was an auspicious time—precisely the moment when interest in "alternative realities" (principally by way of drugs and Eastern mysticism) was at, or nearing, its height. There were relatively few literate Americans, we may be sure, who had not by then heard about Timothy Leary's experiments with LSD, and, at least in the counterculture, there must have been few who had not heard of R. D. Laing, Ken Kesey, and other proponents of alternative realities. Also, 1968 was the year when Tom Wolfe published *The Electric Kool-Aid Acid Test*, his journalistic account of Ken Kesey's acid culture, and Carlos Castaneda published *The Teachings of Don Juan,* an account of a native Amerindian tradition in which peyote and other drugs are used as means to mystical insight and ecstasy. *In Watermelon Sugar* was the third in the year's trilogy of books that were required reading in the counterculture for those who believed that we no longer needed to see things the way that we had been taught to see them and that what we had learned to call "reality" was only one version, and not necessarily the best version, of the world around us.

Brautigan's book has been seen as a fable, a parable, and a work of science fiction, but, above all, it is, as its early readers knew, a tract or treatise, the literary lineage of which may be traced back to far less accomplished works—the religious tracts popular in the nineteenth century. These pamphlets—and if *In Watermelon Sugar* were printed in small type with two or three times as many words to the page, a pamphlet is what it would look like—were distributed by evangelical groups as simple and expedient ways of making their points of view known. Typically, the tract demonstrates its point of view with a brief, simple narrative, sometimes followed by a brief analysis or series of biblical texts that support the points made in the narrative. Remove this "back matter," so to speak, and we have the format for *In Watermelon Sugar.*

Tracts are derived, in general form, from parables but tend to be less schematic and more explicitly directed to the concerns of their contemporary readers. But they never lose sight of the fact that their specific justification is to teach a Christian point of view.

With this is mind, *In Watermelon Sugar* takes on special interest as a tract for our post-Christian era and as a guide to, if not salvation, at least survival. The road to Christian salvation, we are told, begins when we turn our backs on the world about us, and that is exactly what the good people in Brautigan's novel have done. They have taken all the violence, evil, and cruelty of civilization and shut it and its history away, forever, in the Forgotten Works.

Chapter Six
Ennui at the End of Time

Gentle in America

Most of the central figures in Brautigan's fiction published in the 1970s are literally "gentlemen." They wish no one harm; they are passive and withdrawn. They often understand well the world around them, but they are usually too gentle, too passive to criticize, let alone change, it. Much of the interest in these novels lies, for us, in the distance between the corruption that these men find in the world and the disengaged, detached, nonjudging way in which they deal with it—or, as is more likely, fail to deal with it.

These men have little to tell about themselves; their lives seem to have little definition or color. It is as if, having nothing special to do, they just waited silently until their lives were at last linked to circumstances they never anticipated or imagined. Yet there is no sense of surprise and no sense that they have been unfairly treated. However bizarre and improbable those circumstances (which in fact are often very bizarre and very improbable), these men remain utterly passive. Things happen to them, but they do little or nothing to alter their situations.

They sound, of course, very much like Jesse in *A Confederate General from Big Sur* and the narrators of *Trout Fishing in America* and *In Watermelon Sugar*; but, in fact, the situation in Brautigan's novels from the 1970s is very different. For one thing, the narrators of the earlier novels have a kind of strength that is thoroughly lacking in the narrators and other central figures of the later books. The narrator of *Trout Fishing in America* finds much that he does not like—but he is *never* victimized by what he finds. The situation in the later books is very different. Here, the narrators and other central figures are, sooner or later, inevitably victimized. They do not have Lee Mellon's determination to build his world the way he wants it. Sometimes the people in the later books—like C. Card in *Dreaming of Babylon*—may dream, but their dreams are ludicrous. We laugh at him and his dreams, but we would never have laughed at Lee Mellon and his dreams, no matter how emotionally or morally bankrupt they might seem.

The men on whom Brautigan concentrates in his fiction from the 1970s must also be distinguished, in their gentleness and passivity, from the narrators of *Trout Fishing in America* and *In Watermelon Sugar*. Those men were equally gentle and passive, but these qualities kept them outside conventional society; they became observers, watchers, men uniquely in a position to see society panoramically in a way that the rest of us, intimately involved with day-to-day concerns, cannot. But the people with whom Brautigan is concerned in the later novels are, however much against their wills, involved with societal matters, and consequently, in their gentleness and passivity, they are ready victims.

It is true that their special position gives them an ability to see and feel things that the rest of us cannot, and as a result, Brautigan's novels from the 1970s have real interest, but it is never the interest of the earlier fiction. In the end, we are liable to be much less interested in losers—no matter what they have to teach—than in men like Jesse, who understand the extent of evil in the world and who, we are certain, will, nonetheless, survive.

Innocence and Emptiness

The losers in Brautigan's novels may have less interest for us than the men who concerned him earlier, yet there are aspects of these losers which deserve attention. For one thing, they are so gentle, so incapable of aggressive action of any sort, that they literally cannot be changed; they are immutable and, therefore, incorruptible. They are eternally innocent, and if we do not agree with them, we never doubt their honesty. We trust them implicitly. If we find their inability to alter their lives comic and pathetic—much as the tramp in Charlie Chaplin films is comic and pathetic—we also know that, in their innocence, they will not deceive us; we doubt that they would even know what deception is.[1]

In the long run, however, people like this will probably interest us less than someone like the narrator of *Trout Fishing in America*, who is not blinded by innocence. After the visionary intensity of a book like *In Watermelon Sugar,* the clownishness of *The Hawkline Monster* and *Dreaming of Babylon* is disappointing. We have learned to expect so much from Brautigan that we are not liable to be satisfied with yet another silly innocent, forever tripping over his own shoelaces.

"The Literature of Exhaustion"[2]

Brautigan shares with many writers from the 1960s a sense of civilization as having been exhausted or as winding down, approaching its final entropic end. There is, of course, nothing new here (as Jesse would be quick to point out); its literary ancestry in this century goes back to Henry Adams's *Education,* T. S. Eliot's "The Waste Land," and Ernest Hemingway's early fiction, but for later writers, there is a resignation in the face of that exhaustion—less a need to define or characterize it (which, after all, is what men like Adams were doing) than to find ways to survive it.

Kurt Vonnegut, John Barth, Donald Barthelme, and Thomas Pynchon share with Brautigan this sense of entropy—a word as central as any in the literature and criticism of the 1960s—but none was willing to suggest as an antidote anything so drastic as Brautigan's: the total eradication, disaffiliation, or at least retreat of the self from a civilization without a future.

It is interesting here to compare Brautigan with Barth, the man responsible for labeling the literature of this period "The Literature of Exhaustion." In Barth's story "Lost in the Funhouse," a boy named Ambrose goes with his family to Ocean City (Maryland), where they plan to visit the funhouse. During the story, the narrator frequently interrupts himself, first to describe ways of building a story and then to criticize how he is doing it.

Ambrose, meanwhile, decides that someday he will create funhouses like the one at Ocean City, although if he were the sort of person he would like to be, he would not make them—he would just visit and enjoy them. He would, that is, not detach himself from experience—planning the mazes, the special effects—he would enter in and take pleasure in them. Unlike the narrator, busy criticizing his story as he creates it, Ambrose, if he could, would not stand aside and analyze things; he would experience them directly. We know, however, that, even if he cannot do that, he can still create his own world, his own funhouses. Imagination is his salvation—but it is second best.

Brautigan's gentlemen, on the other hand, have sacrificed even Ambrose's birthright: the ability to imagine a new world and then create it. All that they can do is watch and let things happen to them. Neither Ambrose nor Brautigan's gentlemen can be participants, entering into and enjoying life, but Ambrose is saved from this emotional wasteland by his imagination.

Similar comparisons could be made between characters in Brautigan's novels from the 1970s and characters in books by Vonnegut or Barthelme or Pynchon. However bleak experience seems in fiction by these men, it does not reach the point where their central characters are as close to complete withdrawal from experience and understanding as Brautigan's are. In Pynchon's *The Crying of Lot 49,* for example, Oedipa Maas spends her efforts on a literally pointless search for information that, as far as we know, she never gets, but the interesting point here is that although her search is clearly hopeless, she does not stop looking. One of Brautigan's gentlemen would no doubt abandon the search before it really began, and this would be equally true of the earlier, more interesting Brautigan narrators and central figures. Faced with seemingly impossible odds, the Brautigan hero would, like the narrator of *Trout Fishing in America,* finds a comfortable bench in Washington Square or, like the narrator of *In Watermelon Sugar,* study the weather.

Thomas McGuane has written a series of novels about men who are driven into corners from which they can find no immediate escape. They are rendered very nearly as powerless as Brautigan's gentlemen, but in the end, they fight back—and in the process give their author material for something very different from a "literature of exhaustion." An understanding of the way McGuane's fiction works can help underscore the reasons Brautigan's fiction in the 1970s inevitably seems minor.

Revenge Is One Way Out

McGuane's popularity was greatest about the same time as Brautigan's, the late 1960s and early 1970s, and they were popular with the same audience, the counterculture. Although both portray experience in our time as being disjunctive and morally relative, they react to that experience in very different ways. While Brautigan's heroes passively withdraw from the world and watch the chaos pass by, McGuane's respond, often out of great despair, with drugs, nightmare visions, and violence.

In McGuane's *Ninety-Two in the Shade* (1973), to cite his best and best-known work, the central figure, Thomas Skelton, returns to his home in Key West and meets there Nichol Dance, a man of uncompromising violence and unlimited capacity for revenge. Skelton is a casualty of the counterculture, a man who has apparently swallowed the whole pharmacopia of recommended "mind expanding" drugs only to find despair, not heaven. At home in Key West, he might be able to see things clearly again—or so it seems until he meets Dance. Dance owns a fishing boat, and, in revenge for a macabre practical joke, Skelton destroys it. Skelton plans to get a boat for himself and, like Dance, earn a living taking tourists on fishing trips, but Dance, seeking his own revenge now, threatens to kill him if he tries it.

The book is a portrait of violent America—an America in which men like Lee Mellon are in charge. This is the land that produces violent aberrations like Charlie Starkweather, who after all, McGuane suggests, wanted to be a normal boy in the 1950s manner, nice and tough, with a pretty girl beside him in his fast car. And when he couldn't get what he wanted, he hit out at other people. In McGuane's America, a man does not turn the other cheek when he is told that he does not measure up; he hits out and destroys. After Dance fulfills his promise and shoots Skelton, one of Skelton's customers takes his own revenge and bashes Dance's head to jelly. The violence spirals on until there is nothing left to destroy or be destroyed.

Skelton, out on his boat, at one point passes a drive-in theater showing a Civil War movie. Gigantic, screen and movie soar above a camp of mobile homes—the technological refuge for would-be pioneers. These Americans are fascinated and held captive by images of war, and war and its opportunities for violence give them and Skelton, too, an emotional intensity and conviction that, the novel suggests, is characteristically American. But this intensity and conviction are things that Brautigan's gentlemen would, of course, never feel. Like the narrator of *In Watermelon Sugar,* they would, in their passive with-drawal, endure much but never feel anything with the intensity and conviction that McGuane's heroes do. It is in great part this ability to feel deeply and strongly that, on the whole, gives McGuane's people greater or richer interest than Brautigan's.

The Limits of Violence

American obsession with violence is also the subject of McGuane's *Panama* (1978). The emotionally violent, burned-out hero is Chester Hunnicut Pomeroy, a sometime rock star whose stage show, "The Dog Ate the Part We Didn't Like," is the special thrill of rock addicts who want their heavy metal mixed with smoke bombs and gore; it is a live version of *The Rocky Horror Picture Show*—all show and no horror. The trouble, as the book suggests, is that eventually Pomeroy and his American friends will not settle for a theater of violence; they will want the real thing.

Pomeroy gets more than his share of violence—inner, psychological violence. His particular hatred, from which his show is, like drugs, only a relief, is for his father, who has somehow, inexplicably humiliated him, perhaps not least by becoming a highly successful entrepreneur of "leisure foods." Pomeroy's family is descended from violent American heroes—among his ancestors is Jesse James—but there are no heroes of that sort left, and so Pomeroy has created his brutal stage version, a public nightmare, in place of the real thing on a western frontier.

Pomeroy goes too far; the horror that is theater for his audience is real for him. He has tried to relieve the horror with drugs but has only made his nightmares worse. The age of heroic violence is gone, and the violence that is left is locked inside himself. In that situation, only drugs and despair make sense, and so when Pomeroy drops some of his precious cocaine on the sidewalk, he falls to his knees and, ignoring the spectacle that he has become, snorts the drug through a straw he picked up at McDonald's.

Pomeroy is obviously as cut off from the conventional world as any of Brautigan's gentlemen, but although cut off, he has not retreated into that detached, disengaged, and perfectly passive sensibility that they share.

Similarly, Patrick Fitzpatrick, the hero of McGuane's *Nobody's Angel* (1981), returns from his tour of duty as a tank captain in Europe shocked to find his family and town in Montana in a moral and emotional chaos. The Old West is in the hands of people out to make a quick buck. The book ends with Patrick, deeply sickened by what he has found, leasing the family ranch and exiling himself to Madrid. He never, McGuane tells us, returns to Montana.

Confronted with a violent world or one that has been emotionally and morally debased, McGuane's people react in ways very different from the ways in which Brautigan's react. McGuane's people take action of some sort; they are never merely passive, and they are occasionally redeemed by anger and the need for revenge. They are intensely, even painfully, alive, while Brautigan's gentlemen generally let the world pass by. A McGuane character is certainly liable to be a far less pleasant person than one of Brautigan's—though a man like Patrick Fitzpatrick is above all charming—but a McGuane character at least retains a tremendous will and so can act and be, within the social fabric of fiction, a far more interesting and complex man to watch.

Exhausted Technique

Brautigan's gentlemen are of special interest either when, as in *In Watermelon Sugar*, they suggest through their point of view certain metaphysical possibilities or when, as in *A Confederate General from Big Sur* and *Trout Fishing in America*, they suggest new ways of understanding experience and history. But when neither their point of view nor their observations are of interest, Brautigan's fiction at times fails hugely.

A case in point is *Revenge of the Lawn* (1971). Most of the short stories and anecdotes in this book are first-person narratives set in the Northwest and the San Francisco bay area. Some of the pieces are anecdotes recollected from childhood; others involve hippie life in San Francisco. None is more than temporarily amusing or interesting.

The title story, which deals in part with the narrator's grandmother's front lawn and the (supposedly) funny and unexpected things that happen there, is mildly diverting but instantly forgettable. It is the sort of piece that, in its general outlines, one might expect to find in a book like *The Egg and I* by Betty MacDonald—a funny story, that is, about eccentric or rural people during the Depression. Popular literature thrives on such things; they provide diversion without raising difficult questions. Diversion, however, is just about all that they provide.

In Brautigan's story, we learn that the narrator's grandmother, a former bootlegger, had a live-in friend named Jack, who conducted a private war with her lawn. He felt that somehow it was his enemy, and whether or not it was, twice when he was going to park his car there, he overshot his mark and rammed the car into the house. There is more to the story that this, of course, but ultimately we realize that what we have been reading is without special sense or purpose. The story is mildly amusing or diverting, but from Brautigan we have come to expect much more.

None of the stories in the volume seems especially remarkable or especially inventive or complex. Most, like the chapters in Brautigan's novels, are quite short, some less than a page in length. (One has two sentences.) Occasionally there are curious or interesting narrative propositions—as is the case in "Homage to the San Francisco YMCA." This is the story of a man who replaces the plumbing in his house with poetry: Emily Dickinson replaces the kitchen sink, Michael McClure replaces the hot water heater, and minor poets replace the toilet. When he tries to reinstall the plumbing, the poets rebel, and he is forced to move into the YMCA. The idea for the story is interesting and suggestive: what does happen, after all, when poetry becomes as practical as plumbing, as necessary to life as the kitchen sink and the toilet? Another writer might have taken the burlesque to amusing lengths, but it is only the skeleton of a story that we get here.

Some phrasings and metaphors in these stories are reminiscent of Brautigan's better fiction: "She became the theater where he showed the films of his sexual dreams," ". . . he looked as if the only mail he had gotten in his life were bills," and so forth.[3] These occasional fine touches are not enough, however, to relieve the general tedium. In general, the book has little to give it continuing interest.

Of particular interest in this connection are two chapters from *Trout Fishing in America,* which Brautigan says he had lost and so did not include in the published novel. He later rewrote them and published them here. (They were earlier published in a magazine, but after the novel was in print.) He suggests in a note, however, that since he is no longer the person he was, the rewritten chapters are probably in a style very different from the rest of the book. In fact, the rewritten chapters are stylistically flat, dull. There is little to relate them to the rest of the book; the published *Trout Fishing in America,* is, when examined attentively, so clearly seamless, so delightfully and coherently organized, that it is indeed impossible to find a place where these chapters might fit.[4] The first of these chapters, "Rembrandt Creek," is about a stream that looks like a painting. The other, "Carthage Stream," is about a stream that dried up but whose demise has been recorded in photographs in a local newspaper. Both chapters are vaguely—very vaguely—about nature transferred to art: a painting in "the world's largest museum" in one case, photographs in the other. Certainly we see here the kind of unexpected associations that we find throughout *Trout Fishing in America,* and in this sense we can say that the chapters properly belong in the finished novel. But where—and to what end? At other points in the novel, Brautigan's narrator concerns himself with the illusions created by, and the documentary effect of, photographs and other works of art. (The opening chapter is a case in point.) But what intrigues us is the way in which the information or the anecdote is conveyed, the narrator's point of view. But the point of view is missing in the rewritten chapters, and the tone is flat. We have an interesting comparison, but that is far from enough to make interesting literature.

When *Revenge of the Lawn* was published, Brautigan's popularity was at its peak. A reviewer for the *New Republic* noted that the book was "the height of fashion right now,"[5] and it surely was: at parties during the winter of 1971–72, *Revenge of the Lawn* was one of *the* books to discuss.

But not every critic, despite the book's popularity, was prepared to say kind things about it. *Kirkus Reviews* said that the book could have been called " 'Little Abortions' since none [of the stories] really seems to come full term even by the loose standards Brautigan sets."[6] In the *New Yorker,* Garrison Keillor delightfully parodied Brautigan's rather primitive and minimal (rather than minimalist) effects in these stories. "Ten stories for Mr. Richard Brautigan," he wrote, "are nothing. He never eats lunch until he's thought up 110."[7]

Demotic Style

A far more interesting book, although surely not by any means as fine as Brautigan's earlier fiction, is *The Abortion: An Historical Romance 1966* (1971)—a mildly amusing, inoffensive, but, on the whole, bland novel about a San Francisco librarian who has an affair with a beautiful woman, gets her pregnant, and takes her to Tijuana for an abortion. It is somewhat longer—226 pages in the original edition—than many of Brautigan's works, but the length is not justified. There is too little here to sustain any great interest. As a short novel, it might have succeeded. Certainly it has more intrinsic interest than the stories in *Revenge of the Lawn,* but there is little to warrant more than a casual reading.

Like other Brautigan novels, *The Abortion* makes a great show and celebration of "sensitivity." The narrator—who, like the narrators of *Trout Fishing in America* and *A Confederate General from Big Sur,* is unnamed—is so sensitive and so passive that we can only marvel at his ability to manage the day-to-day business of living. In spite of his sensitivity, however, the narrator seems quite incapable of any deep sympathy for, or understanding of, others. Emotionally, he seems very nearly empty, sterile.

He runs a library where unrecognized and unpublished writers can store their books. It is surely a very American enterprise—a place where the common man, any man at all, can get a (very small) measure of recognition. It does not matter how poorly or how well he writes; all that matters is that he writes. The library exists as an ultimate statement of the belief that all men—or at least all writers—are created equal. There is no favoritism here. Any writer can have his book in the library, although, of course, this is no guarantee that the book will ever be read, and in fact, we learn that eventually all the books are stored in caves where, alas, they are subject to water damage. No one could read them even if he wanted.

The narrator takes his job quite seriously. The library is scheduled to be open only from nine in the morning until nine at night, but he stays there all the time: you never know when the common man will finish his book and decide to give it to the library. Among the books which the librarian receives are a volume by a little boy about his tricycle, a book about leather (written on leather) by a motorcyclist, a cookbook dealing with food in Dostoyevsky's novels, a seven-volume history of Nebraska, and "Richard Brautigan's" own contribution, a volume titled *Moose*.[8] Presumably none of these books will ever be read, but their authors can be assured that their work and their names will, more or less, be preserved. No one may recognize a certain author's name, but it will survive, nonetheless, in a card catalog that no one consults.

Josephine Hendin has argued that "Brautigan is a spokesman for the disenchanted, seeking to allay anxiety by blurring the distinctions of status, wealth, and ambition which exist in the real world."[9] It is true that in his novels published in the 1970s, everyone gets a chance to succeed, although usually in trivial ways and at what, in Miss Hendin's "real world," would seem a terrible cost. "The distinctions of status, wealth, and ambition" are quite blurred in Brautigan's fiction published in the 1970s, but at the same time the emotional relationships and satisfactions that a man might get from these distinctions are also blurred or gone, and there is nothing new in their place. The library in *The Abortion* may offer a kind of salvation for literary failures—it always has more shelf space—but it offers no real sympathy or understanding for the people who make use of it. True, the "real world" may have ceased to exert its repressive and critical powers, but the cost may be prohibitive. There is a deadly chill at the heart of this world.

Having forced aside the narrow expectations and limits of civilization, Brautigan's central figures in his novels from the 1970s find themselves not strengthened, not emotionally enriched and free, but rather emotionally hollowed, unable to love or hate with any great subtlety, depth, or passion. Nor—and this is the ultimate issue, the point at which their emotional and moral bankruptcy becomes clear—do they care. There is no sense of frustration or rage, no sense of having been outrageously cheated, and there is no intimation—as there is in the earlier novels—that the loss of a rich moral, emotional, and private life has for its compensation a greater spiritual and historical awareness or sensibility. The men in the novels from the 1970s may entertain us briefly with their innocence and clownishness, but, unlike their predecessors, they do not take us down into the engine rooms of absolute reality in order that we may better understand how and why it works.

Demotic Vision

The heroine of *The Abortion* has a beautiful body (in the *Playboy* manner) and one desire—that men pay less attention to her body than to *her.* What she looks like is not, she says, what she is. Her name is Vida Kramar; she looks like her first name but would prefer to look like her second. A walking centerfold, she would, if she could, go unnoticed. And so, if she cannot go unnoticed, she can at least live with someone who can—the librarian. It is apparently just the sort of relationship that she wants: cold, impersonal, and dull. He provides her with the anonymity that she desires; the forgotten books do not whistle at her or call her names. On the other hand, the librarian is pleased, very pleased, to find a real centerfold in his life.

The anonymity that Vida wants and that the librarian offers has much in common with that utter lack of aggressive identity that so many of Brautigan's narrators and other characters cultivate. The loss of such an identity would, according to the narrator of *In Watermelon Sugar,* be a very good thing, but the narrator-librarian in *The Abortion* does not agree that anonymity or passive withdrawal from life would be a good thing for *Vida.* Indeed, if she were plain, passive, and anonymous, the narrator would almost certainly not look at her twice.

There is here a moral contradiction that makes *The Abortion* an especially bleak novel. Whether or not it was Brautigan's intention, the novel undercuts the moral direction of his earlier fiction. The destruction of the self that in *In Watermelon Sugar* leads to special aesthetic, spiritual, and political awareness leads in *The Abortion* to aesthetic, spiritual, and political aridity—a bleak moral plain on which one is supposed to be exactly what others expect and want. It is a deeply conservative, conformist solution.

The problem lies in an altogether too facile acceptance of popular culture and its premises about human behavior. This acceptance is not merely a means of locating commonly shared myths with which to structure fiction—the role which it plays, for example, in such major counterculture books as Ken Kesey's *One Flew Over the Cuckoo's Nest* and Robert Pirsig's *Zen and the Art of Motorcycle Maintenance*[10]—but rather an acceptance of these popular myths as something of significance and interest in themselves. The point of *The Abortion* may be that Vida should *want* to be the centerfold that others say she is; and to arguments that this is an obvious and cruel form of depersonalization, we should remember that depersonalization—although of a very different type— is what most of Brautigan's fiction, good and bad, is all about. Unexpectedly and unpleasantly, the depersonalization of popular culture becomes a kind of salvation, a shortcut, perhaps, to Nirvana. But that conclusion may find little appreciation in Benares or Kyoto. What the librarian wants from Vida is, in its social ramifications, far more inhuman than he may realize.

The narrator-librarian sits in the abortionist's office and, despite the fact that he never really approves of the abortion, does nothing to stop it. He could never bring himself to act in a willful fashion. He lacks all but the rudiments of a will; whatever his moral perceptions, he is not able to act on them except in his library. When it is necessary to arrange for the abortion, he turns to a friend for help. Why should not Vida, then, be the same—totally passive, dependent on others even for her sense of herself, even if that sense is ultimately derived from popular culture?

The need for total passivity and acceptance is very much part of Zen training and vision, of course, but it ceases to make sense when that passivity and acceptance lead not to a profound understanding of experience but to the obvious victimization and trivialization of a popular commercial culture. And at that point we have good reason to think again of the massive differences that separate East and West.

Narcissism or Nirvana

One of the most attractive aspects of Buddhist thought lies in its insistence that the man who seeks Nirvana will be deeply compassionate toward others. The narrator-librarian of *The Abortion* obviously expresses a concern for those whose literary efforts will never be cataloged in the Library of Congress, but it is a type of concern that requires people only in the abstract. The librarian does not really know the people for whom he feels this concern—he does not even read their books. This is emotion without risk; there is nothing to lose.

Nothing, that is, if he does not leave his post. When he abandons his job—temporarily, he thinks—to take Vida to Tijuana, he returns to find his job usurped. Without his job, he has nothing to do except collect money for the organization that sponsors the library. He is outside *everything* now; there is no apparent cause for his concern or his compassion. He could, morally and emotionally, focus more on himself, less on others.

There is obviously a vast difference between, on the one hand, the mystic vision of Zen with its acceptance of things as they are and compassion for those who suffer and, on the other, the passive narcissistic vision of the world as merely a context for one's self. It is the narcissist's vision which we find in the narrator here. None of the narrators of Brautigan's earlier fiction, except Jesse, showed much compassion, but they were not so entirely withdrawn from human contact and possibility as the narrator-librarian. Both the Zen mystic and the narcissist may withdraw from the world, but while the former returns with a profounder sense of its workings, the latter gains only a kind of hermetic self-protection. Like the narrator-librarian, he is emotionally self-sufficient, or largely so, and he is alone. In pathological form, narcissism involves a man's folding in on himself so much that he is unable to act decisively, to express himself satisfactorily, and to deal in any but the most primitive emotional fashion with the world. Other people are not seen in their complexity but in a comic-strip simplicity, the terms of popular culture.

If America in the 1970s became a narcissistic culture, as Christopher Lasch and others have argued,[11] then the narrator-librarian is only an extreme of a common type—namely, the man who derives identity and emotional satisfaction, such as it is, from himself. It is a psychological terrain as dreary, sordid, and emotionally antiseptic as the abortionist's office in Tijuana. We recoil from *The Abortion*'s personal and social implications; its narrator is not, cannot be, on any road to enlightenment. He has withdrawn into himself so far that, unlike the narrator of *Trout Fishing in America,* he can show us nothing useful about the historical world we share. He has nothing to show us finally but the dead cold that lies at the heart of the narcissistic self.

For all its apparent similarities with Brautigan's earlier novels, *The Abortion,* when compared with them, is so cold and so narrow in its political and moral vision that a poor critical reception should have been expected. On the whole, however, critics who did not like the book expressed their dissatisfaction in general ways; they were less concerned perhaps with what the book said than with the fact that it obviously did not measure up to the standard set by the earlier novels: it was not as well written; it was less complex; and so forth.

In the *New York Review of Books,* Robert Adams wrote an exceedingly complimentary review of Brautigan's earlier novels but concluded that although *The Abortion* "isn't a bad book, it just isn't much of a book,"[12] and in the *New York Times,* Thomas Lask wrote that ". . . the substance of 'the Abortion' is thin to the point of invisibility."[13] One English critic felt that as an exercise in creative writing, it might get a C minus.[14]

Surely the book is better than that—but it is a vast distance from the earlier novels. Indeed, not until *The Tokyo-Montana Express* was published nearly a decade later was there another Brautigan book with the interest of *A Confederate General from Big Sur, Trout Fishing in America,* and *In Watermelon Sugar.*

Sombrero Fallout

American fascination with the self, the narcissistic self, leads, as Lasch and others have indicated, to a national moral and emotional impoverishment. Emerson, Thoreau, and Whitman looked for an autonomous American imagination, but it was not this kind of autonomy they sought—an autonomy, that is, with no social or moral responsibility. This narcissistic solitude ends not in Emerson's cosmic visions but in a dull, narrow, and shallow self.

The narcissist's little world, established outside history and social commitment, can be found in *Sombrero Fallout,* perhaps the least of all Brautigan's novels. Published in 1976, the year in which Americans were celebrating two hundred years of individualism and independence, the novel shows the dark side of that individualism.

The novel concerns a man, unnamed, who is transfixed by, of all things, a strand of hair left behind by his Japanese girl friend. His commitment to everything else in life—except himself and the strand of hair—is about as minimal as it could be. He is alone with himself, and the girl friend, who sleeps and dreams through the novel, is in effect as divided from any world of shared experience as he is. At the same time, a story that the narrator has begun but then thrown out starts magically to write itself. (It is, for once, all very "whimsical"— that adjective with which reviewers have repeatedly tried to pigeonhole Brautigan's books.) The story concerns a sombrero that lands, out of nowhere, on a village street in the Southwest and, by some mysterious power, eventually starts a riot.

At times, the book is amusing, but its social and psychological implications are not. Like *The Abortion,* it deals largely with people who are emotionally and morally shut into themselves, not with people who, like the narrator of *Trout Fishing in America,* would take vast extents of time and culture as their province. What is interesting is that the private, closed-in world of the narrator is passive, while the rest of the book—at least the part involving the story that is writing itself—is aggressive, violent, and cruel.

We have here a variation on a typical Brautigan dilemma: a passive hero and a violently aggressive world. There are similarities here with, for example, Jesse's situation at Lee Mellon's place and with the narrator's situation at the ritual suicide of inBOIL. But in the earlier books we are asked to understand the violent world in the terms, or through the perspective, of the passive observer, whereas in *Sombrero Fallout* we are shown the two as absolutely cut off from each other. The two are set side by side; nothing welds them together. There is, as Emerson knew, little value in solitude itself; it is rather what solitude allows us to see that is of interest.

Thomas McGuane's fiction provides a helpful contrast here. The heroes in his novels—men who react to a hostile, violent world by challenging it, even when the challenge inevitably leads to death—are, if not necessarily more admirable than the solitary man in *Sombrero Fallout,* at least more complex, more liable to attract interest. Solitude may be for many an inevitable fact of contemporary life, but that will not make it inevitably interesting. *Sombrero Fallout,* which, it should suprise no one, has generated a good deal of negative criticism, is a book that seems as dull and empty of purpose as its hero.

Chapter Seven
Resting in Space

The Landscape

Although Brautigan's novels published in the 1970s are generally weaker than his other fiction, they have some interest as comments on popular culture, especially popular fiction and films. *The Abortion,* as we have seen, is thematically linked to matters of popular culture, and while *Sombrero Fallout* is not, *The Hawkline Monster* (1971), *Willard and His Bowling Trophies* (1975), and *Dreaming of Babylon* (1977) are parodies of popular literary and film genres—pornography, gothics, westerns, and hard-boiled detective stories.

None of these books approximates the achievement of the earlier works, yet some critics may have dealt with them too harshly. Several critics have treated these books favorably—sometimes quite favorably—but negative comments are not hard to find. One commentator with a sense of humor claimed that *The Hawkline Monster* had "its moments but one is not likely to remember them,"[1] while Roger Sale in the *Hudson Review* called it "a terrible book, deeply unfunny, in no need of having been written."[2] Peter Ackroyd in an especially biting review in the *Spectator* told his readers that ". . . fortunately, the novel is arranged as a series of brief chapters, and the print is very large, so the tedium of its self-indulgent whimsy is camouflaged for quite long periods."[3]

Well, it is not quite *that* bad. Like *Willard and His Bowling Trophies* and *Dreaming of Babylon*, *The Hawkline Monster* has both its comic moments—although perhaps a good many fewer than its author intended—and insights into the popular genres that it parodies.

Mapping the Terrain

The popular genres which Brautigan parodies celebrate the sort of private narcissistic dreams shared, we may assume, by readers or at least remembered from childhood and adolescence. Whether as cowboy or detective or stud or valiant hero, the central figures in these books and films provide their readers with conflicts and possibilities that few of us are liable to find in day-to-day life. "In that well-known and controlled landscape of the imagination," John G. Cawelti has said, "the tensions, ambiguities, and frustrations of ordinary experience are painted over by magic pigments of adventure, romance and mystery. The world for a time takes on the shape of our heart's desire."[4] In other words, the world becomes in effect a projection of our desires, and heroes succeed much as we would like ourselves to succeed if things were what we secretly wish they could be.

This is also an ideal terrain for narcissism, for if there is one thing a narcissist cannot do it is to admit that he is incapable of doing what he set out to do. Identifying with the hero of a work of popular culture—whether it be *Conan* or *Flash Gordon* or *Star Wars* or *The Big Sleep* or *Reds*—assures him of eventual victory and at no risk to himself or his reputation.

Cowboys and Flower Children

The Hawkline Monster parodies westerns and gothics—not those gothic romances, written for women, which have long been a staple of bookracks in supermarkets and drug stores, but rather gothic horror films in which mad scientists discover magic potions and create monsters. In literature, the type can be traced back to Mary Shelley's *Frankenstein* and Robert Louis Stevenson's *Dr. Jekyll and Mr. Hyde,* but it is the filmed versions of these books and their successors—films robbed of much of the original moral purpose—that Brautigan parodies.

The novel takes place in 1902—an appropriate time for a parody of a western, since the first best-selling western published by a major house, Owen Wister's *The Virginian,* had appeared the year before and the prototypical western film, *The Great Train Robbery,* was released the year after. But only the date is right; everything else is, in some way or other, bizarre.

Two gunslingers named Greer and Cameron are hired to hunt down and destroy a monster created by a mad scientist. Cameron is distinguished by the fact that he counts—he counts everything available, including the number of gunshots he hears, the number of times he throws up, and the number of women named Hawkline that he meets. There are two of these women, twin sisters, one of whom, under the monster's influence, spends a brief period as "Magic Child," an Indian maid who, to the amazement and delight of the men she meets, considers their pleasure her special province. She is something of an ur-hippie, an early flower child, but while she is somewhat out of place on the frontier, men greet her with some enthusiasm, and understandably she spends much of her time in bed.

Magic Child's father, Professor Hawkline, is the mad scientist responsible for creating the monster, which in turn has turned him into an umbrella stand. The monster lives in a cave beneath the Hawkline mansion, where the cowboys finally destroy it. The professor is restored to life, but his house is accidentally destroyed by fire, and the site is engulfed by a lake. The monster is turned into diamonds.

If all this sounds like very silly stuff, it is. There are amusing passages in *The Hawkline Monster,* and, as a short story, it might have succeeded, but as a novel, it is far too long, its characterizations too thin, and its plot too trivial for sustained interest. The fault belongs in part to the genres being parodied, particularly the film gothic; there is not much in the original to parody, but Mel Brooks's *Young Frankenstein* was able to do much more and do it with far more wit.

The novel's value, such as it is, lies in its implied criticism of certain stereotypes in popular culture. If *The Abortion* is able to find value in such stereotypes, *The Hawkline Monster* ridicules them. Greer and Cameron, his counting excepted, sound like the cowboys we know from books and movies. Hawkline's accidentally created monster is in a direct line from movie monsters of the 1930s, but when the monster and the gunslingers are brought together, they reveal themselves for the absurdities that they are. The spectacle is amusing to watch, but it could have been done, with considerably less tedium, in a short story.

Flagellation for Fun

Willard and His Bowling Trophies parodies sadomasochistic books of which *The Story of O* is the best known example. In Brautigan's novel, a young couple have turned their sex life into the kind of sadomasochistic nightmare that presumably exists only on the outermost fringes of the conventional world. Neither partner is seriously hurt in their games, however—which is perhaps Brautigan's point: they are only playing with cruelty and pain. But they find out soon enough how trivial their games are; they are shot by men who have mistaken them for intended victims.

We have no sympathy for the couple; as pictured by Brautigan, they are so monstrously, thoroughly involved with their private perverse selves that they no longer have any public identity. In a way, they are a comment on other Brautigan people, like the librarian in *The Abortion*—people, that is, who are shut into their private fantasies and have left no room for affection or compassion.

The point is interesting and important, and the actual killings are made to seem inevitable, horrifying, but somehow just. But once again, we are dealing with a book much too long for what it accomplishes. The ending is truly shocking and effective, but the road we have to travel to get there is far too long.

The Gentle and the Tough

Dreaming of Babylon is much more interesting and successful as a parody than either *The Hawkline Monster* or *Willard and His Bowling Trophies*. The earlier parodies deal with only a few of the most obvious characteristics of the genres they parody, but *Dreaming of Babylon* does much more.

The novel is set in the land of the hard-boiled detective story, where things, in terms of our everyday world, can seem simply silly. Women spend much of their time in bed if they are young, and drinking gin if they are not. Men who are not "pansies" beat their enemies into a bloody pulp but get up each morning with huge headaches from drinking or from fights the night before. The novel usually includes one or more "sun-drenched" urban landscape or a street scene at night in the rain with streetlamps reflected in the wet pavement. There is usually a scene or two indoors with the sunlight glowing through pulled shades or a flashing neon sign outside alternately lighting up the room and plunging it into darkness. Everything in this world is somehow sleazy or seedy. And that is part of its pleasure: we get to see things that we would never see in our conventional world.

The hard-boiled detective trusts no one—he cannot; even the cops are corrupt. Nor can he trust women; they are good for a little sex but not much else except—to put it in a typically hard-boiled way—a little decoration.

In real life, as Raymond Chandler said, a private eye "has about as much moral stature as a stop and go sign,"[5] but in fiction, he is redeemed by a primitive moral code based on a sense of duty to his employers. He will kill if he has to, but he will never betray his employers. Money, in other words, is more important than anything else; it is at the foundation of the moral code, such as it is, shared by hard-boiled detective fiction.

Aside from the detective himself and a primitive moral code, the principal characteristic of this kind of fiction is its tone or style, which is blunt and visual. It is this which explains why hard-boiled detective fiction is so reminiscent of movies and in turn had such a large effect on them, especially gangster films such as those that Warner Brothers produced in the 1930s and the *film noir* works of the 1940s. Dashiell Hammett's *The Maltese Falcon* and Chandler's *The Big Sleep* are so intensely visual that they read like scenarios fleshed out into books.

Although the tone is set largely by this intense visual emphasis, there is also a characteristic literary style shared by most authors of this type of book. The prose is generally lean, spare, and taut except for occasional extravagant adjectives and metaphors. Brautigan's prose can also, of course, be described this way, and in fact his diction shares much with that of the masters of hard-boiled detective fiction, especially Chandler, and that is one reason why this genre was especially appropriate for Brautigan to parody or imitate. The point can be best demonstrated by listing phrases from the two authors:

1. The gravestones "were small boards that looked like heels of stale bread."[6]
2. "Blood began to move around in me, like a prospective tenant looking for a house."[7]
3. "The sunshine was as empty as a headwaiter's smile."[8]
4. Hitchhiking, "I would stick out my thumb as if it were a bunch of bananas."[9]
5. The dead man's body "was leaking blood like those capsules we used to use with oleomargarine. . . ."[10]

6. "The eighty-five cent dinner tasted like a discarded mail bag. . . ."[11]

The second and third examples are from Chandler's *The Big Sleep*; the last, from *Farewell, My Lovely*. The others are from *Trout Fishing in America*. The similarity in tone as well as sheer outrageousness of metaphor should be obvious.

The people in Brautigan's novels are often trapped in places very much like the imaginary world of the hard-boiled detective story—places, that is, where few can be trusted and where paranoia is only common sense. *Trout Fishing in America* describes an America that idolizes "Pretty Boy" Floyd and other criminals, and inBOIL, the villain of *In Watermelon Sugar,* makes Chandler's villains look gentle by comparison. In most of Brautigan's fiction, violence is inevitably present, often barely suppressed, waiting for the right moment to break out.

The detective in *Dreaming of Babylon* is C. Card (Calling Card? Seek Hard?), gentle, detached, and uninvolved, but no less aware than other hard-boiled detectives of how cruel and violent the world around him can be. The difference is that where others of his type would shoot now and ask questions later Card does as little as possible, which is often nothing at all, to protect himself. He merely watches the havoc and destruction around him, but the book suggests that, paradoxically, the effect can be as devastating as aggression and violence.

Dreaming of Babylon

It is 1942, and C. Card is a private detective in San Francisco, where his profits are low and his rent is overdue. (He is happy, naturally, when his landlady dies, for he knows it will be a good while until her estate is settled and someone comes around to collect his overdue rent.) He is not exactly prepared for his job: his major problem at the beginning of the book is finding bullets for his gun.

Card dreams of Babylon, a place where wishes come true, a place where he can be a great baseball player or anything else that he wants. And it is a good thing that Card has dreams: he has no women friends and little ambition, but in his dreams, he can get anything he wants, especially women. Poor Card: he failed his entrance test for the police force because he was dreaming of Babylon, but what else could one expect from a man who cannot remember to put on both socks and who was wounded in the Spanish Civil War because he was not looking at what he was doing and sat on his gun? (That war, Hemingway knew, was a fine testing ground for men, hard-boiled and otherwise, but Card went because he thought he might find something there that looked like Babylon.) Nothing Card has done has ever worked out quite right. He is a loser's loser.

But Card is surrounded by people who are as tough as any villain or cop in a Warner Brothers movie or Dick Tracy comic strip. Sgt. Rink of the local police force is a really tough cop; he could, we imagine, crush Card's skull without really trying. And there is Peg-leg, who runs the city's morgue; he is also tough and, at the beginning of the book, eager to show his latest acquisition, a pretty whore who has been stabbed in the back. The other tough characters include a rich, attractive woman who drinks vast quantities of beer without ever, to Card's astonishment, going to the bathroom.

The rich woman hires Card to kidnap (for reasons never explained) the whore's body from the morgue, but she also (again for reasons unknown) hires others to do the same. Card succeeds and hides the body in his refrigerator, but the woman is arrested by Sgt. Rink, and Card is left at the end of the novel with nothing with which to pay his rent except a body in the icebox.

The story, of course, makes no sense, and *it is not supposed to.* Questions are purposely left unanswered. Why does the rich woman want the body? What will Card do with it now that he has it in his icebox? It does not matter at all; in true hard-boiled detective-story form, even the crucial riddles can be left unsolved—or, if solved, done in such an intricate, eccentric, and complex fashion that even a very attentive reader, having read the solution, might have difficulty restating just what the solution was.

The solution to a mystery in a hard-boiled detective story is so much less important than the creation of atmosphere and character that even the most important plot details may be obscurely passed over, the most essential questions left unanswered. Trying to state concisely what happens in *The Maltese Falcon* might have taxed Hammett himself. In

Chandler's *The Big Sleep,* a character named Owen Taylor is murdered, and the discovery of his body is graphically described, but the reader never learns exactly why Taylor was killed, and apparently Chandler never knew himself. When the oversight was spotted—after thousands had read the book and never, it seems, noticed the detail or at least publicly commented on it—Chandler had to admit that he did not have the foggiest notion how to unravel the mystery; he had forgotten all about it. But his oversight has not barred the novel from continued popularity.

What is important in the hard-boiled detective story, we have seen, is the tone or mood, particularly the mood created by the sense that anyone here can be trapped in a bizarre maze of seeming coincidences—justification for rampant paranoia. What matters is not so much the explanation for the maze—the solution of the mystery or crime, that is—as the detective's tough, uncompromising attitude which allows him to survive it. We are attracted to the fact that he is self-assured, aggressive, and tough, because it appears to be these characteristics, not providence or chance, which allow him to win. We are reassured that the individual, even a poor hack like the private detective, can survive on his own wits. But the special thing about Card is that, despite the fact that he has none of the traditional characteristics of the hard-boiled detective, he, too, wins. If he winds up with a body in his refrigerator, that is not his fault; he did exactly what he was paid to do, and it was his employer who made the mistakes.

And so a typical Brautigan gentleman survives and succeeds again. Card, of course, is a joke, and he is far from, say, Jesse's gentle wisdom in *A Confederate General from Big Sur.* But there may be a greater similarity between Jesse and Card than we might guess at first glance. There may well be a kind of strength in gentleness (as the narrator of *In Watermelon Sugar* might say) and strength in the private imagination, even when that imagination does nothing but dream impossible things. Whether or not this has application or meaning in our conventional world, it is central or implied throughout most of Brautigan's fiction.

Dreaming of Babylon and Brautigan's other parodies have, as we have seen, modest literary value, but they have marked problems and are simply not as ambitious or accomplished as his earlier fiction. They are entertaining in a mild, inoffensive way, and we should not be surprised that they have generally sold well. Nonetheless, they bear a relation to *Trout Fishing in America* that, for example, Mark Twain's *Tom Sawyer* bears to *Huckleberry Finn*. *Dreaming of Babylon* and *Tom Sawyer* are interesting but certainly not major books; it is *Huckleberry Finn* and *Trout Fishing in America* to which we repeatedly return, reassured with each reading that we are dealing with imaginatively and morally complex and accomplished works of fiction.

The Other Side of the Coin

Before turning from Brautigan's fiction published in the 1970s, we should look briefly at the work of Tom Robbins, whose considerable reputation as a comic novelist was early established, like Brautigan's, in the counterculture. Robbins's novels, more than the novels of any other popular writer of the time, are an expression of the counterculture's iconoclastic attitudes toward everything from films to philosophy, rock to religion. But while Robbins's books are as quick as Brautigan's to satirize conventional middle-class ideas and attitudes, Robbins's celebrate other ideas and attitudes that a typical Brautigan narrator might determinedly and darkly view from a distance.

Brautigan's narrators are, on the whole, so far from the center of middle-class American experience, so unlike anything that might be considered conventional, that they could never be absorbed into the mainstream of American life. Their alienation and solitude are inevitable. But in Robbins's work, solitude and alienation are gone and have been replaced by a kind of gentle affection, a diffused love for all things. There are few hostilities, although many misunderstandings, in Robbins's fiction. In Brautigan's books, people have a difficult time *happily* surviving anything, but in Robbins's, people not only survive happily—they also set out to save the world.

In spite of differences between them, Robbins seems to have learned much from Brautigan. When we find in Robbins's fiction metaphors like "an epistolary style that rattles and wobbles like a loose head lamp on a Hell's Angel's hog" or of grass covered with frost and looking "as if it had been chewing Tums" or of sun that "warmed his chest like a Vapo Rub," we are dealing with extravagant metaphors that are Brautigan's special sign.[12] *Trout Fishing in America* is also referred to in *Another Roadside Attraction,* the first and, to date, the best of Robbins's novels.

Amanda and the Mushroom

Amanda is the heroine of *Another Roadside Attraction*. She is just the sort of woman that the 1960s should have produced but seldom did—the ultimate flower child. There are five things that Amanda likes best: mushrooms, motorcycles, butterflies, cacti, and the Infinite Goof, prosaically known to others as the riddle of the universe. Famed for her marijuana breads, a connoisseur of mushrooms that do exciting things to her mind, Amanda will not accept the world as it is; it must and will become—if necessary, with the aid of a drug or two—exactly what she wants. She is an extraordinarily optimistic and resilient person, and when the frequent and heavy rains at her new home in the state of Washington make a motorcycle impractical, she is consoled by the fact that the dreary climate is perfect for 2,500 varieties of mushrooms. One *learns,* Amanda knows, to be happy,[13] and Amanda is a very happy woman.

Amanda operates a rather unique roadside attraction, the Capt. Kendrick Memorial Hot Dog Wildlife Preserve (vegetarian foods, no preservatives, no soft drinks), where she also dispenses wisdom about the universe. Amanda lives life like a butterfly (one of the things she admires), experiencing the world and making it beautiful but never trying to dominate it.

Brautigan's narrators, particularly the narrator of *Trout Fishing in America,* also accept the world as they find it; outside of their dreams and their imaginative visions, there is not much that they can do to change it. But if a person cannot change the world, he can change himself and the way he views things and that is exactly what Amanda does. She says that in the end, nothing matters—there's nothing really to lose or gain—so one should simply be as happy and free as one wants.[14] Whatever place history has devised for Amanda, she can, like Jesse and Lee Mellon, imagine herself to be anything she wants—even a butterfly. Amanda's salvation is Amanda's business.

But Amanda is far more happy and blithe about that salvation than a Brautigan character might be. Life, she believes, can be sweet and grand as long as the only authority you obey is your own. The flaws in the sweetness come from concessions, compromises, and, above all, the willingness to believe that someone knows better than you. Amanda, like Brautigan's characters, would rather be alone than compromise, but, unlike them, she speaks with infectiously bright optimism. Amanda speaks—or spoke—for a very self-assured generation. The narrator of *Trout Fishing in America* is alone; he has no followers, and he asks for none. But Amanda is a new messiah with, so it seemed when the book was published in 1971, a whole nation, the Woodstock nation, following in her wake.

Conceivably, if Amanda's persistent optimism ever ran out, she would find the imaginative and emotional sterility that threatens all of Brautigan's narrators when they cut themselves off from society and particularly when they cease to observe others and, as in *Sombrero Fallout,* observe only themselves. Amanda, in other words, could someday learn with swift terror the emotional implications of her belief that there is really nothing to lose or gain—so do what you want.[15] Experience might then seem closer to what is evoked in a work by Samuel Beckett than that curious amalgamation of situation comedy and fairy tale that we find in *Another Roadside Attraction.*

If Robbins's novel is superior to Brautigan's parodies, it is, nonetheless, true that Brautigan's characters are somewhat more aware than Robbins's that the world can be a very unpleasant place in which to live. Amanda is somewhat too blithe and genial in her outlook on things, we may feel. Charming though she is, her chances of surviving the world at large might be substantially increased if she were to cultivate a little healthy paranoia. The solipsistic reveries of C. Card and other characters in Brautigan's parodies may be better protection agains the world than Amanda's charm and naiveté.

But, strangely enough, it may also in part be that charm and naiveté that make *Another Roadside Attraction* a superior book. C. Card's solipsistic reveries are in effect an admission that he is, after all, just one more loser, and while Amanda's view of experience is narrow and unrealistic, it provides an energy and enthusiasm that drives her and the novel along at white heat. If we could choose between an evening with Amanda or an evening with Card, there would perhaps not be much question about which we would take.

Chapter Eight
A New Land, Much Like the Old
Sunrise in the East

This book began at Monterey, California, with a festival of music—and the political values that accompanied it—that had a profound effect on the rise of the counterculture. And those values, we found, had much to do with the popular appreciation—and, at the same time, deep misunderstanding—of Brautigan's fiction in the late 1960s and early 1970s. The counterculture, above all, preached shared, communal values—a fact clearly evident in the very idea of a "Woodstock nation"—and such values have little room in Brautigan's work. To have assumed, as did so many in the counterculture, that he or rather his works were "like us" or, for that matter, like anything that had come before was to misconstrue deeply the purpose and achievement of both the fiction and the poetry.

Robert Adams was right when he claimed, in his review of the early fiction, that these books were, strictly speaking, not novels—they were too special for that. As a matter of convenience and convention, critics and readers will undoubtedly continue referring to them, as we have done, as novels, but Adams was right in suggesting that, all things considered, they had best be grouped together simply as "Brautigans."[1] There is a determined independence about everything Brautigan has written that resists traditional, formal labels.

It may be helpful now to move forward to a very different occasion and a generation with values very different from those popularized by "the summer of love." This newer generation might not understand Brautigan's work any more than the counterculture did, but at least they would not give anyone cause to label him, in the words of *Time*, "an honorary kid" or, in the words of *Life*, "the gentle poet of the young."[2]

The place this time is not California but New York, where, sooner or later, all American writers, even determined western writers, must come to find publishers and/or good reputations—at least publishers and reputations with more than local significance. In 1980, Brautigan, who had spent much of the preceding eight years in Japan and on his ranch near Livingston, Montana, embarked on a lecture tour in conjunction with the publication of his new book, *The Tokyo-Montana Express,* and one of his major stops was in New York. This was, he said, the first time since 1974 that he had been farther east than Billings, Montana.

And much had changed in the interim. By 1980, there was in effect no counterculture—as Brautigan could have confirmed merely by looking out over the audience of students, academics, and well-dressed professionals who had come to hear him read as part of a very staid and very famous series of poetry readings sponsored by the 92nd Street YM-YWHA. Brautigan, wearing his denim shirt, dungarees, and cowboy boots, may have looked slightly out of place among his more conservatively dressed listeners—but the differences here were not important. It was, after all, Brautigan's work, not Brautigan, that interested his attentive listeners. He found an audience that was reserved, respectful, and sympathetic and that was far more interested in what he had decided to read than, as might have been the case with an earlier audience, what he was said to represent.

And that, of course, was all for the good, for if Brautigan were to survive as a writer of distinction, it would have to be, sooner or later, because of what he wrote rather than because of his place in the past. That this new audience was willing to take Brautigan on his own terms was an encouraging sign indeed.

Furthermore, the book that he had just published, *The Tokyo-Montana Express,* was a far better work than any of his books published in the 1970s. It is without the puzzling moral ambiguities and vacuous characterizations that lessen our interest in *The Abortion, The Hawkline Monster,* and other novels that he published in that decade. The diction in *The Tokyo-Montana Express* is as lean, spare, and effective as that in the early fiction, but the tone is moderate, restrained, almost delicate. There are fewer characteristic Brautigan metaphors than in *Trout Fishing in America*—the book which *The Tokyo-Montana Express* most resembles, but the typical Brautigan narrator—solitary, withdrawn, but fundamentally content even when threatened by the world around him—is again at the center of the book.

The Tokyo-Montana Express is apparently drawn from Brautigan's experiences in Japan, San Francisco, and Montana. We have noted the profound implicit effect which Japanese culture in general and Zen Buddhism in particular has had on his work. Here the influences become explicit. If the book is "about" anything—and at first it may seem nothing more than a miscellany of anecdotes and observations from the narrator's life—it is about two very different cultures, East and West, American and Japanese, and their effect on each other. *The Tokyo-Montana Express* is Brautigan's "Passage to India," but the passage turns out to be a well-traveled highway with much traffic and exchange of goods, both physical and metaphysical. He finds the values of the East thriving in Montana, and the values of the West doing a rich business in Japan.

The book has 131 short chapters dealing with a vast variety of what may seem, on first reading, totally unrelated topics: taking a walk in the snow, seeing a beautiful Japanese woman on a train in Tokyo, purchasing a humidifier in Montana, watching a Japanese erotic movie and missing the ending (and then going back the next day and discovering that the theater has literally disappeared), and so on. Unrelated though the chapters may seem at first, they prove, on second reading, to be, much like the chapters in *Trout Fishing in America*, linked closely, that is, in metaphor, tone, and subject. *The Tokyo-Montana Express* is not as tightly, if eccentrically, knit as the earlier novel, but the structural parallels between the two are obvious. In the later book, we find the same grouping of chapters according to miscellaneous subjects—food, for example, or the weather—while other, more abstract concerns repeatedly surface throughout the book: friendship, communication, suicide, solitude, and so forth. Within any of these groups or series of chapters, Brautigan tends to alternate between, on the one hand, anecdotes and observations related geographically and/or culturally to Japan and, on the other, those related to America, especially California and Montana.

First-Person Singular

"The 'I' in this book," says Brautigan's narrator, "is the voice of the stations along the tracks of the Tokyo-Montana Express" (vii)[3]—a statement which, despite its interest as a literary conceit, is not liable to make much sense to many readers. There is, of course, no real Tokyo-Montana Express, with or without stations along the way, and for that matter, little of the book has anything to do with travel. The conceit refers rather to metaphysical travel in the trade of ideas between West and East.

The ideas exchanged are not, however, those which easily lend themselves to explanation in textbooks. Here as always, Brautigan centers on ideas that, in common everyday language, would be inexpressible, ineffable. We have seen how, in his early works, he devised metaphors of a special sort—indeterminate, vague, but highly evocative—to convey ideas that cannot be discussed in everyday language, and we find this technique here, although to a lesser degree. His narrator tells us, for example, that fishing tackle stores were "cathedrals of childhood romance, for [he] spent thousands of hours worshipping the possibilities of rods and reels that led like a religion to rivers and lakes waiting to be fished in the imagination . . ." (27).

But there are fewer metaphors here than in the earlier work. Instead, to convey, as well as he can, the special meanings that he is trying to refine, Brautigan emphasizes the narrator's perspective much as he does in *In Watermelon Sugar*. This allows him to illuminate things with a clarity that many of us may never find elsewhere.

There is neither complexity nor tension in the narrator's life and in his special vision. He is perfectly at peace with himself; there is little anxiety or unsatisfied desire here; and so he can stand impassively and tell us things that, in the rush and confusion of our private lives, we would ordinarily overlook. He is, above all, a man whom we can trust. Even when we do not agree with him, we have no sense that he is deceitful or dishonest, and, a very welcome trait, he also has a nice sense of humor:

I feel no anxiety to go home because I am alone. When I get home an empty bed in a hotel room waits for me like a bridge to lonely and solitary sleep.
So I just stand there as peaceful as a banana because that's what I look like in this all-Japanese crowd (21).

The worlds described and occupied by many Brautigan narrators and central figures in such lesser novels as *The Abortion* and *Sombrero Fallout* are largely solipsistic; essentially these men offer us inventions of the private imagination, quite unrelated to the world that most of us presumably recognize and share. In these lesser novels, a world is invented as a substitute for one that is both more real and vastly more threatening. When C. Card feels uncomfortable with the people around him, he dreams of Babylon and so shifts into a world that he, not they, controls.

But in the best Brautigan books—of which *The Tokyo-Montana Express* is certainly one—escape is not that easy. Their narrators may, like all of us, have their private reveries, but eventually they are brought up short, faced with people, customs, and desires outside their control. Since their narrators are usually withdrawn, private people, they have no friends to whom they can turn—none, at least, who are close. The narrator of *Trout Fishing in America* refers to his daughter and his "woman," and the narrator of *The Tokyo-Montana Express* talks about his Japanese wife, but neither narrator characterizes these members of his family—people whom, we would assume, he should know nearly as well as he knows himself. Whatever their relationships, these people remain distant and abstract; they do not even have names. But while these narrators have no close friends, they do not devise dream worlds to entertain and satisfy themselves—nor do they allow themselves to be changed by the expectations and values of others. They know, in Emerson's words, that "Nothing is at last sacred but the integrity of [one's] own mind,"[4] and if the price for this is solitude, it is a price which they *never* hesitate to pay.

What we have then in *The Tokyo-Montana Express* and other major Brautigan fiction is an absolute integrity that is neither solipsistic nor self-indulgent—nor, for that matter, an integrity ever justified with the sort of moral rhetoric which Emerson, Thoreau, and other nineteenth-century Americans used to support their determined individualism.[5] The narrator of *The Tokyo-Montana Express* has passed beyond the need for justification; secure in a Zen-like certainty, he knows that he sees the world as it is: certainly violent and threatening but also, in the final order of the universe, inconsequential and even a little silly. Just as the narrator of *Trout Fishing in America* is able to view peace marches with amusement, the narrator of *The Tokyo-Montana Express* is able to laugh—although never unkindly—at the remnants of the hippies, utterly incongruous in a world that has almost forgotten that such people ever existed (94–97, 123–125).

East and West

The first chapter of *The Tokyo-Montana Express* concerns a nineteenth-century immigrant to America, Joseph Francl, a well-educated, ambitious musician from Czechoslovakia.[6] Why he came to America is the question that the chapter asks but is never able to answer satisfactorily. In America, Francl sets off to find gold in California, but all that he finds, alone on the frontier, is stillness, solitude, silence, and ultimately death. He keeps his dreams of success to the end but realizes none of them.

But if we will never know why Francl gave up a cultivated European life to come to America, his experience may suggest what, whether as immigrants or native-born Americans, the rest of us can expect. There are many references to, and accounts of, American seekers in *The Tokyo-Montana Express*—especially aging and ineffective hippies—but nobody is capable of finally getting anything for his efforts. The America described by Brautigan is a place of solitude and silence, the things which men must expect if they obey the national imperative and dream of individual freedom. Francl perhaps dreamed of the freedom that he could buy if he discovered gold, but in a profound, metaphysical way he was already, in his solitude on the frontier, as free as any man ever was: free of politics, free of society, free of history. The only question left is whether that freedom is worth the terrible human and emotional price that it demands. The answer to that is implicit throughout *The Tokyo-Montana Express*—a narrator who never compromises his freedom and never regrets his decision to stand alone. The things in life that he seems to enjoy are the same things that most of us enjoy—good food, good movies, and good sex—and sometimes all that he wants from the rest of his life, he says, is "a little mindless fun" (74). He is no Joseph Francl searching for gold and other phantoms; he is utterly realistic and contents himself with what he already has.

The narrator's freedom involves a renunciation of the world and a willing acceptance of the solitude that this renunciation entails. It is an act that we would more likely expect in the East than the West. But nothing in a Brautigan book turns out to be just what we would expect, and here, just as the East is found in the West, so is the West found in the East. The Tokyo that the narrator describes is a city of factories, automobiles, trains, hotels, and money—never Zen solitude and contemplation.

In a chapter entitled "Kyoto, Montana," the narrator compares a famous Japanese Buddhist shrine with a landscape near his ranch in Montana. The shrine is more than six hundred years old; however beautiful and religiously significant it is, it comes to us from a past long dead. But the landscape in Montana, free of history and civilization, can be seen in the present moment for what it is; we do not need a historian or a theologian to interpret it for us. The shrine—the Moss Garden in Kyoto—is, to begin with, a kind of artifice, while the landscape in Montana is natural; shaped by geology, not man. If a man were to obey the Buddhist injunction to renounce the world and find, through that renunciation, spiritual awareness and wisdom, would he not be better off in America, or certain parts of America, rather than surrounded by the industry and artifice of historical and modern Japan?

There are many references in the book to artificial, electronic forms of communication—telephones, televisions, and so forth—and the final chapter describes a teletype in Tokyo beginning its daily work. The chapter and the book end with the words of the teletype, inhuman and mechanical:

:ATTENTION SUBSCRIBERS:
GOOD MORNING

The teletype, artificially binding the world together, typing East to West, is metaphysically as well as geographically at the opposite end of the world from Montana. It would be easy to be snared into believing, as we have seen happen in *The Abortion,* that the impersonality of a commercial culture has something important in common with the impersonality of the Buddhist ideal of solitude and separation from conventional civilized values and expectations. But the point of apparent similarity, impersonality, is finally neither very meaningful nor interesting. The difference between them—namely, the fact that the second requires human will and perception—is what matters, and *The*

Tokyo-Montana Express, which, like all of Brautigan's best fiction, evolves from the point where the world and an individual's special mode of perception meet, has no use for electronic gadgetry—except perhaps convenience, entertainment, even "a little mindless fun." In themselves, however, these inventions are valueless; the narrator in his solitude has found much of greater interest and value: "These mountains of Montana are endlessly changing, minute to minute, nothing remains the same. It is the work of sun and wind and snow. It is the play of clouds and shadows.

"I am staring at the mountains again" (19).

We should recall here the ending of *A Confederate General from Big Sur,* where Jesse, having freed himself from history and social obligation, stands on the shore of the Pacific, faces the East, and confronts the paradox of a universe that is simultaneously both eternally changing and eternally the same. Similarly, the narrator of *The Tokyo-Montana Express* looks out at the mountains near his home and, on the one hand, sees something that is as permanent as anything of this world ever was but that, on the other, is "endlessly changing." It is in such moments of illumination that the narrator's special perspective, particularly his renunciation of civilization, is justified and fulfilled.

Resolution and Resignation

The Tokyo-Montana Express is a mature expression of a narrative perspective developed throughout Brautigan's best work. It is not structurally or narratively as complex and, therefore, as interesting as *Trout Fishing in America* and, in parts, is trite—even, alas, whimsical.[7] Some of the chapters in *The Tokyo-Montana Express* are as lightweight and casual as many of the pieces in *Revenge of the Lawn.* In its way, the novel bears a relation to Brautigan's earlier work similar to the relation that Whitman's "Passage to India" (1871) bears to "Song of Myself" (1855): the later work may not measure up to the earlier, but has importance both in its own right and as an expansion of thinking that the earlier began.

The narrator of *The Tokyo-Montana Express,* like Jesse and the narrators of *Trout Fishing in America* and *In Watermelon Sugar,* find calm and understanding by, so to speak, standing on the banks of civilization and fishing it for all that it is worth. But they never step into the stream where the current could sweep them away. They choose to be the fishers, not the fish.

But their decision, as we have seen, is no easy one, and it should not surprise us if their books are repeatedly said to be self-indulgent, solipsistic, even whimsical. By their very stance, which is less rebellious than simply resigned, these men must offend those who take their historical selves seriously and insist that the rest of us do also.

It is impossible to predict where Brautigan's literary interests will take him next, but *The Tokyo-Montana Express* does suggest a return to the type of book Brautigan does best, the type of book which earned him his initial critical and popular success. It may be that he has come full circle, leaving behind the less promising terrain of literary parody.

Brautigan may never duplicate the success of *Trout Fishing in America,* but the special vision developed there, and evoked again in *The Tokyo-Montana Express,* has, we may hope, not exhausted itself. But even if Brautigan never again approximates his early success, he should find himself with a very high place indeed in the estimation of those concerned with the development of American literature in our time.

And Finally

The four major Brautigan books—*A Confederate General from Big Sur, Trout Fishing in America, In Watermelon Sugar,* and *The Tokyo-Montana Express*—are characterized first by their resigned opposition to convention and custom of any sort. At close range, such things appear to be, after all, only the milder forms of tyranny.

Brautigan's books, read properly, sketch out a vision of freedom in America. The autonomous self which the early novels evoke is seen in *The Tokyo-Montana Express* to be in fundamental ways at least as American as it is Eastern. Perhaps it would not always have seemed that way, but as the East "improves" itself through modern technology, freedom and autonomy—particularly freedom from systems, intellectual as well as political—find their ideal home in the vacancy of the American West. The Zen experience had its origins in the East, but, insofar as it has a geographic home, it may now seem at least as appropriate to this side of the Pacific as to the other.

In his own way, Brautigan returns us to the question that Emerson once asked: "Why should not we have a poetry and philosophy of insight and not of tradition, and a religion by revelation to us. . .?"[8] But this requires a freedom from history and tradition, and it is this that Jesse ultimately realizes, and it is with this realization that the other major Brautigan works begin.

Notes and References

Preface

1. John Barth, quoted in "How's Fiction Doing," *New York Times Book Review,* 14 December 1980, p. 3.

Chapter One

1. There were, of course, a variety of disparate interests and people in what we call the "counterculture." The committed political activist was not necessarily the same person who experimented with drugs or the person who spent his time and money on the concerts and recordings by the Jefferson Airplane. Nonetheless, Brautigan's reputation seemed to span the entire movement, although, as we will discuss, political activists had special reservations about his work. Nonetheless, while he was being treated with suspicion or contempt in some established literary journals, he could anticipate a warm reception in counterculture magazines as different as *Ramparts* and *Rolling Stone.*
2. Hunter S. Thompson, *Fear and Loathing in Las Vegas* (New York: Popular Library, 1971), pp. 178–79.
3. Christopher Lasch, *The Agony of the American Left* (New York: Knopf, 1969), passim.
4. Anonymous, "The Message of History's Biggest Happening," *Time* 94 (29 August 1969):32–33.
5. Malcolm Muggeridge, review of *A Confederate General from Big Sur, Esquire* 63 (April 1965):60.
6. Anonymous, review of *A Confederate General from Big Sur, Playboy,* March 1965, p. 22; Philip Rahv, review of *A Confederate General from Big Sur, New York Review of Books,* 8 April 1965, p. 10.
7. John Skow, review of *The Abortion, Time* 97 (5 April 1971):24.
8. Jonathan Yardley, "Still Loving," *New Republic* 164 (20 March 1971):24.
9. Jill Krementz, photograph of Richard Brautigan, *New York Times Book Review,* 14 September 1975, p. 4.
10. Anonymous, review of *Sombrero Fallout, Choice* 13 (January 1977):1433.
11. Robert Christgau, review of *Sombrero Fallout, New York Times Book Review,* 10 October 1976, p. 4.

12. Anonymous, review of *The Abortion, The Times Literary Supplement,* 2 February 1973, p. 113.

13. Michael Feld, review of *In Watermelon Sugar, A Confederate General from Big Sur,* and *Trout Fishing in America,* London Magazine 11 (August/September 1971):150.

14. Yardley, "Still Loving," p. 24.

15. Anatole Broyard, review of *Revenge of the Lawn, New York Times,* 15 November 1971, p. 39.

16. Robert Adams, "Brautigan Was Here," *New York Review of Books,* 22 April 1971, p. 24.

17. Cheryl Walker, "Richard Brautigan: Youth Fishing in America," *Modern Occasions* 2 (1972):308–9.

18. Yardley, "Still Loving," p. 24.

19. John Clayton, "Richard Brautigan: The Politics of Woodstock," *New American Review* 11 (1971):67.

20. Tony Tanner, review of *Trout Fishing in America, The Times,* 25 July 1970, p. 5.

21. John Ciardi, quoted on the back cover of the Delta edition of *Trout Fishing in America* (New York, 1969).

22. Tom McGuane, review of *Trout Fishing in America, The Pill Versus the Springhill Mine Disaster,* and *In Watermelon Sugar, New York Times Book Review,* 15 February 1970, p. 49.

23. Adams, "Brautigan Was Here," p. 24.

24. Jim Langlois, review of *The Abortion, Library Journal* 96 (15 May 1971):1726.

25. Ron Loewinsohn, "After the Mimeograph Revolution," *TriQuarterly* 18 (Spring 1970):229. Loewinsohn, it should be noted, is one of the two men to whom the book is dedicated.

26. Walker, "Richard Brautigan," p. 313.

27. R. Z. Sheppard, review of *Revenge of the Lawn, Time* 98 (1 November 1971):114.

28. The literature in English on Zen Buddhism has grown enormously in the past two decades, but for those unacquainted with the subject, the best introductions are still those provided by D. T. Suzuki's *Essays in Zen Buddhism,* 3 vols. (London: Luzac, 1927, 1933, 1934). A selection of Suzuki's writings can be found in *Zen Buddhism: Selected Writings,* ed. William Barrett (Garden City, N.Y.: Doubleday, 1956). See also R. H. Blyth, *Zen and Zen Classics,* comp. Frederick Franck (New York: Random House, 1978). This is a selection of writings by an English admirer of Japanese and Zen culture who began to study Zen long before the subject was known, even by name, to much of the Western world.

29. Brautigan discusses briefly his interest in Zen in the introduction to *June 30th, June 30th* (New York, 1978), pp. 1–11. Brautigan also read some of his poetry as part of a discussion of "Zen and Contemporary Poetry" with Gary Snyder, Philip Whalen, Robert Bly, and Lucien Stryk at the meeting of the Modern Language Association in San Francisco in December 1979.
30. Bruce Cook, *The Beat Generation* (New York, 1971), p. 208.
31. Ibid.
32. A comment made with emphasis at a lecture and reading which Brautigan gave on 24 November 1980 at the 92nd Street YM-YWHA, New York City.
33. Cf. Jonathan Williams, review of *Rommel Drives on Deep into Egypt, Parnassus* 1 (Fall/Winter 1972):100. Among Williams's comments: "There is less here than meets the eye," and Brautigan "writes for kids who eat macrobiotic food and (don't) know where it is. . . . you'd starve to death on these no-cal poems." Thomas McGuane (review of *Trout Fishing in America*, p. 49) said of *The Pill Versus the Springhill Mine Disaster* that "Without the fictions to refer them to, they would seem to be merely bad poems."
34. Strongly recommended as an introduction to poetry of this sort, particularly the influence of Williams and Kerouac on it, are *The Poetics of the New American Poetry*, ed. Donald Allen and Warren Tallman (New York: Grove Press, 1973), and the lectures and interviews collected in Allen Ginsberg's *Composed on the Tongue*, ed. Donald Allen (Bolinas, Calif.: Grey Fox Press, 1980).
35. *The Galilee Hitch-Hiker* (San Francisco, 1958) is out of print, but the poem appears in *The Pill Versus the Springhill Mine Disaster* (New York, 1968) together with "1942" and "The Nature Poem," portions of which are quoted below. These two poems were earlier published in *The Octopus Frontier*, which is also out of print.
36. Among important discussions of the insubstantiality or impermanence of Brautigan's metaphors is Charles Russell's "The Vault of Language: Self-Reflective Artifice in Contemporary American Fiction," *Modern Fiction Studies* 20 (Autumn 1974):349–57.
37. Cf. Tony Tanner, *City of Words: American Fiction 1950–1970* (New York, 1971) and Jerome Klinkowitz, *Literary Disruptions: The Making of a Post-Contemporary American Fiction* (Urbana: University of Illinois Press, 1975).

Chapter Two

1. *A Confederate General from Big Sur* (New York, 1964). Page references in text.
2. Terence Malley, *Richard Brautigan* (New York, 1972), p. 98.

3. Its demise was predicted well in advance in Christopher Lasch, *The Agony of the American Left* (New York: Knopf, 1969).

4. Ecclesiastes 9:11. Even the phrase "neither yet bread to the wise" is literally and humorously suggested in the novel. Immediately preceding the book's first reference to Ecclesiastes, Jesse tells us that Lee Mellon bakes bread that is something less than a delicacy: a hard rock-like substance "like Betty Crocker gone to hell" (69). Eventually Jesse is able to eat it, but until then, there is literally no "bread to the wise."

5. Ralph W. Emerson, "Self-Reliance," *Essays: First Series,* Centenary Edition (Boston: Houghton Mifflin, 1903), p. 50.

Chapter Three

1. Walt Whitman, "Song of Myself," *Leaves of Grass,* ed. Harold W. Blodgett and Sculley Bradley (New York: New York University Press, 1965), p. 32.

2. Ibid., p. 50.

3. The narrator goes fishing, lives in San Francisco, and has a wife and daughter, but aside from such general details, we know little about him. We may understand his special attitude toward experience, but we are given few details from his personal life. He is an intensely private person.

4. F. R. Leavis, *The Great Tradition* (London: Chatto and Windus, 1948), p. 27.

5. There are actually forty-eight chapters if we count an untitled section at the beginning of the book and fifty (as in fifty states?) if we include the two "lost" chapters that were later published in *Revenge of the Lawn* (New York, 1971). Brautigan does not number the chapters, but for our purposes it makes a convenient shorthand to do so.

6. *Trout Fishing in America* (San Francisco, 1967). Page references in text.

7. It is, in fact, so commonplace as to require little comment, but at least one recent study of this phenomenon may be mentioned, Harvey Cox's *Turning East* (New York: Simon and Schuster, 1977), which shows how Oriental mysticism can be, and has been, successfully packaged for American consumption. If even mysticism can be made a salable commodity, it would seem that there must be few limits to what can be packaged and sold in America.

8. Lawrence Ferlinghetti, *A Coney Island of the Mind* (New York: New Directions, 1958), p. 10.

9. Perhaps the genial family doctor in Brautigan's *In Watermelon Sugar* is intended as a quiet homage to the good and charitable man that Dr. Williams is generally said to have been.

10. Henry David Thoreau, *Walden* (Princeton, N.J.: Princeton University Press, 1971), p. 51.

11. Ibid., p. 323.

12. John Steinbeck, *The Grapes of Wrath* (New York: Viking Press, 1939), p. 103.

13. Tanner, *City of Words*, p. 328.

14. Herman Melville, *Moby-Dick*, ed. Charles Feidelson, Jr., (Indianapolis: Bobbs-Merrill, 1964), p. 63.

15. Thoreau, *Walden*, p. 98.

Chapter Four

1. Tom Robbins, *Still Life with Woodpecker* (New York: Bantam Books, 1980), p. 150.

2. Ibid.

3. R. M. Olderman, *Beyond the Waste Land: A Study of the Novel in the Nineteen-Sixties* (New Haven: Yale University Press, 1972), p. 15.

4. D. T. Suzuki, "East and West" in *Zen Buddhism and Psychoanalysis,* ed. D. T. Suzuki, Erich Fromm, and Richard DeMartino (New York: Harper, 1960), pp. 1–6.

Chapter Five

1. *In Watermelon Sugar* (San Francisco, 1968). Page references in text.

Chapter Six

1. Josephine Hendin discusses the gentleness of Brautigan's people in detail in her book *Vulnerable People* (New York, 1978), pp. 44–50. It is an intelligent, provocative discussion, but one with which the present author finds much to argue. In particular, she sees the withdrawal of these people from the world as a "strategic maneuver" to preserve themselves from threatening forces. She may well be attributing the wrong motive; what comes first may be the demands of their particular sensibility, not a desire to protect themselves—that is, a positive, rather than negative, motivation. They would, in other words, withdraw from the world even if it were not threatening. These people seem a good deal less calculating than Hendin's analysis suggests.

2. This title is borrowed from a rather famous essay by John Barth— "The Literature of Exhaustion," *Atlantic Monthly* 220 (August 1967):29–34—in which he argued that contemporary literature had exhausted its traditionally recognized potentials. Accurate or not, the essay was considered

a major statement of the dilemma of post-modern fiction. Brautigan's work, on the other hand, suggested, by its very uniqueness, that literature still offered as yet unexploited possibilities. The debate over Barth's contentions was certainly intense in literary and academic places, but with the passing of time, both the article and the debate it inspired seem to have been forgotten. Nonetheless, the title remains suggestive for discussions of the literature of the time and the critical assumptions that informed much of it.

3. *Revenge of the Lawn* (New York, 1971), pp. 48, 100.

4. Malley in *Richard Brautigan* comes to a similar conclusion. He feels that these chapters are "markedly inferior to most of the material" in the novel and that "they don't fit into the structure of the book at all" (p. 201).

5. *New Republic* 166 (22 January 1972):29.

6. *Kirkus Reviews* 39 (1 August 1971):824.

7. Garrison Keillor, "Ten Stories for Mr. Richard Brautigan and Other Stories" *New Yorker* 47 (18 March 1972):37.

8. A title taken perhaps from Thoreau's somewhat unexpected, and as yet unexplained, last words. If any great American writer deserved space in this library, it would be Thoreau, whose first book, *A Week on the Concord and Merrimack Rivers,* sold only 218 copies in the four years following its publication in 1849.

9. Josephine Hendin, "Experimental Fiction," in *Harvard Guide to Contemporary American Writing,* ed. Daniel Hoffman (Cambridge, Mass.: Harvard University Press, 1979), p. 260.

10. For a study of the uses of popular culture in Kesey's novel, see Terry G. Sherwood, *"One Flew over the Cuckoo's Nest* and the Comic Strip," *Critique* 13 (1971):96–109.

11. Christopher Lasch, *The Culture of Narcissism: American Life in an Age of Diminishing Expectations* (New York: Norton, 1979). Of the many studies of the "me decade," Lasch's seems the best researched and reasoned.

12. Robert Adams, "Brautigan Was Here," *New York Review of Books,* 22 April 1971, p. 26.

13. Thomas Lask, review of *The Abortion, New York Times,* 30 March 1971, p. 33.

14. Susan Hill, review of *The Abortion, Listener* 89 (25 January 1973):124.

Chapter Seven

1. Anonymous, review of *The Hawkline Monster, Progressive* 39 (January 1975):55.

2. Roger Sale, review of *The Hawkline Monster; Hudson Review* 27 (Winter 1974–75):624.

3. Peter Ackroyd, review of *The Hawkline Monster, Spectator* 234 (5 April 1975):411.

4. John G. Cawelti, *Adventure, Mystery, and Romance: Formula Stories as Art and Popular Culture* (Chicago: University of Chicago Press, 1976), p. 1.

5. Frank McShane, *The Life of Raymond Chandler* (New York: Dutton, 1976), p. 70.

6. *Trout Fishing in America,* p. 20.

7. Raymond Chandler, *The Big Sleep* (New York: Random House, 1976), p. 180.

8. Ibid., p. 203.

9. *Trout Fishing,* p. 6.

10. Ibid., p. 88.

11. Raymond Chandler, *Farewell, My Lovely* (New York: Random House, 1976), p. 205.

12. Tom Robbins, *Another Roadside Attraction* (New York: Ballantine, 1971), pp. 182, 33, 22.

13. Ibid., p. 12.

14. Ibid., p. 335.

15. Ibid.

Chapter Eight

1. Robert Adams, "Brautigan Was Here," *New York Review of Books,* 22 April 1971, p. 24.

2. John Skow, review of *The Abortion, Time* 97 (5 April 1971):95.

3. *The Tokyo-Montana Express* (New York, 1980). Page references in text.

4. Emerson, "Self-Reliance," *Essays: First Series,* p. 50.

5. This is a conventional argument, but those who wish to explore its implications further might start with Quentin Anderson, *The Imperial Self* (New York: Random House, 1970). Aspects of the argument as related to Thoreau are discussed in my study of nineteenth-century American romanticism, *The Civilized Wilderness* (New York: Free Press, 1975).

6. This chapter was originally published as the introduction to a limited edition (540 copies) of *The Overland Journey of Joseph Francl: The First Bohemian to Cross the Plains to the California Gold Fields* (San Francisco: W. P. Wreden, 1968).

7. How else could we describe, for example, the chapter entitled "The Smallest Snowstorm on Record," which traces the fate of two snowflakes named Laurel and Hardy?

8. Emerson, "Nature," *Nature: Addresses and Lectures,* p. 3.

Selected Bibliography

PRIMARY SOURCES

1. Poetry

All Watched Over by Machines of Loving Grace. [San Francisco]: Communication Company, [1967].

Five Poems. Berkeley, Calif.: Serendipity Books, 1971.

Four New Poets (with Martin Hoberman, Carl Larsen, and James M. Singer). [San Francisco]: Inferno Press, [1957].

The Galilee Hitch-Hiker. San Francisco: White Rabbit Press, 1958.

June 30th, June 30th. New York: Delacorte Press/ Seymour Lawrence, 1977.

Lay the Marble Tea. San Francisco: Carp Press, 1959.

Loading Mercury with a Pitchfork. New York: Simon and Schuster, 1976.

The Octopus Frontier, San Francisco: Carp Press, 1960.

The Pill Versus the Springhill Mine Disaster. San Francisco: Four Seasons Foundation, 1968.

The Return of the Rivers. [San Francisco]: Inferno Press, [ca. 1958].

Rommel Drives on Deep into Egypt. New York: Delacorte Press / Seymour Lawrence, 1970.

2. Novels

The Abortion: An Historical Romance 1966. New York: Simon and Schuster, 1971.

A Confederate General from Big Sur. New York: Grove Press, 1964.

Dreaming of Babylon: A Private Eye Novel 1942. New York: Delacorte Press / Seymour Lawrence, 1977.

The Hawkline Monster: A Gothic Western. New York: Simon and Schuster, 1974.

In Watermelon Sugar. San Francisco: Four Seasons Foundation, 1968.

Sombrero Fallout: A Japanese Novel. New York: Simon and Schuster, 1976.

The Tokyo-Montana Express. New York: Delacorte Press / Seymour Lawrence, 1980.

Trout Fishing in America. San Francisco: Four Seasons Foundation, 1967.

Willard and His Bowling Trophies: A Perverse Mystery. New York: Simon and Schuster, 1975.

3. Short Stories

Revenge of the Lawn: Stories 1962–1970. New York: Simon and Schuster, 1971.

4. Selected Works

Trout Fishing in America. The Pill Versus the Springhill Mine Disaster, and *In Watermelon Sugar.* New York: Delacorte Press / Seymour Lawrence, 1969.

5. Miscellaneous

Listening to Richard Brautigan. (Recording.) Hollywood, Calif.: Harvest Records, 1970.

Please Plant This Book. (Seed packets with Brautigan poems.) San Francisco: Graham Mackintosh, 1968.

SECONDARY SOURCES

1. Bibliographies

Jones, Stephen R. "Richard Brautigan, A Bibliography." *Bulletin of Bibliography* 33 (January 1976):53–59.

Lepper, Gary M. "Richard Brautigan." *A Bibliographical Introduction to Seventy-Five Modern American Authors.* Berkeley, Calif.: Serendipity Books, 1976, pp. 81–84.

Wanless, James, and Kolodziej, Christine. "Richard Brautigan: A Working Checklist." *Critique* 16 (1974):41–52.

2. Critical and Biographical Studies

Adams, Robert. "Brautigan Was Here." *New York Review of Books,* (22 April 1971), pp. 24–26. A judicious analysis of the early novels, which Adams feels should more properly be called "Brautigans."

Bales, Kent. "Fishing the Ambivalence, or, A Reading of *Trout Fishing in America.*" *Western Humanities Review* 29 (Winter 1975):29–42. Highly personal and enthusiastic response to *Trout Fishing in America.*

Clayton, John. "Richard Brautigan: The Politics of Woodstock." *New American Review* 11 (1971):56–68. Expresses fear that those who adopt the point of view of Brautigan's narrators will withdraw from political commitments.

Cook, Bruce. *The Beat Generation.* New York: Scribners, 1970. Interview with Brautigan and speculations on his place in the Beat movement.

Hansen, Arlen J. "The Celebration of Solipsism: A New Trend in American Fiction." *Modern Fiction Studies* 19 (Spring 1963):5–15. Believes that in Brautigan's fiction, the man shapes his world rather than the other way around.

Hayden, Brad. "Echoes of *Walden* in *Trout Fishing in America*." *Thoreau Society Quarterly* 8 (July 1976):21–25. Shows exactly what its title indicates but overlooks important references to *Walden* in the chapter entitled "The Cabinet of Dr. Caligari."

Hearron, Thomas. "Escape Through Imagination in *Trout Fishing in America*." *Critique* 16 (1974):25–31. The imagination in *Trout Fishing in America* as an antidote to, and means of escape from, modern industrialized, urbanized America.

Hendin, Josephine. *Vulnerable People*. New York: Oxford University Press, 1978. Suggests social and political implications of acting in the manner of typical Brautigan characters—gentle, withdrawn, emotionally distant.

Hernlund, Patricia, "Author's Intent: *In Watermelon Sugar*." *Critique* 16 (1974):5–17. Discusses the emotional repression or deprivation that is necessary for "the gentle life" in *In Watermelon Sugar* to succeed.

Hicks, Jack. *In the Singer's Temple*. Chapel Hill: University of North Carolina Press, 1981. A study of contemporary fiction with emphasis on Brautigan as counterculture writer.

Kern, Robert, "Williams, Brautigan, and the Poetics of Primitivism," *Chicago Review* 27 (Summer 1975):47–57. Compares Brautigan's poetry with William Carlos Williams's in terms of their shared "primitivist poetics."

Leavitt, Harvey. "The Regained Paradise of Brautigan's *In Watermelon Sugar*." *Critique* 16 (1974):18–24. Analyzes the novel in terms of traditional myths; calls the book "the Bible for the contemporary college generation" (p. 24), a verdict no longer true but indicative of the book's former popularity among younger readers.

Loewinsohn, Ron. "After the Mimeograph Revolution." *TriQuarterly* 18 (Spring 1970):221–36. Important historical and critical study of Brautigan's work by a very sympathetic observer.

Malley, Terence. *Richard Brautigan*. Writers for the Seventies Series. New York: Warner Paperback Library, 1972. A fine study, partly dated by its enthusiastic 1960s slant and language but filled with fine insights.

Pütz, Manfred. *The Story of Identity: American Fiction of the Sixties*. Stuttgart: J. B. Metzlersche Verlagsbuchhandlung, 1979. A brilliant book including an extensive examination of Brautigan's concern with the place of the individual in America. Points out important parallels with the Transcendentalists.

Russell, Charles. "The Vault of Language: Self-Reflective Artifice in Contemporary American Fiction." *Modern Fiction Studies* 20 (Autumn

1974):349–57. Discusses the impermanent, fluid nature of Brautigan's metaphors.

Schmitz, Neil. "Richard Brautigan and the Modern Pastoral." *Modern Fiction Studies* 19 (Spring 1973):109–25. Examines myth, particularly pastoral myth, in Brautigan's fiction.

Stickney, John. "Gentle Poet of the Young." *Life,* 19 August 1970, pp. 49–52, 54. Partly significant for data on Brautigan's early life and career but even more significant as a key example of the popular attention Brautigan received as an "honorary hippie."

Tanner, Tony. *City of Words: American Fiction 1950–1970.* New York: Harper and Row, 1971. Brilliant insights into Brautigan's use of language and the place of *Trout Fishing in America* in the development of American fiction.

Vanderwerken, David L. *"Trout Fishing in America* and the American Tradition." *Critique* 16 (1974):32–40. A general study of *Trout Fishing in America.* Emphasizes the importance to the book of the possibilities of the transcending power of the imagination.

Index